Paul H Batt
2018

To: Jen

From: JERI ☺
& Kathy

PRAISE FOR HOW GOODNESS PAYS

"This book on goodness is a timely offering on a timeless topic full of time-tested ideas that will bring renewal and purpose to your leadership and life."

RICHARD LEIDER, INTERNATIONAL BEST-SELLING
AUTHOR OF *THE POWER OF PURPOSE, REPACKING
YOUR BAGS, AND LIFE REIMAGINED*

"Batz has another great book that is simple and profound. He and Paul Hillen have written a book on business that every leader needs to read. They show how goodness pays financially and in so many other ways. Goodness is a timeless idea and the world needs leaders who are aligned with goodness now more than ever."

DAN MALLIN, CEO, MANAGING PARTNER, AND
FOUNDER, EQUALS 3, LLC

"At Qlik, we are a living example of how goodness pays around the globe. The ideas and research communicated in this book are exactly the ways we partner with NGOs, the United Nations, and local non-profits to help them improve their organizations and their outcomes. This book is really about corporate social responsibility, high performance, and how goodness pays in employee/employer relationships to the world we want. And I love it."

JULIE KAE WHIPPLE, GLOBAL HEAD OF CORPORATE
RESPONSIBILITY, QLIK

"Every person has the desire to enjoy a 'good' life. The confidence of knowing you are improving each and every day is incredibly powerful. *How Goodness Pays* is a well-written book that will provide you with clear and concise coaching principles that will make you a more effective person and leader."

KEVIN WARREN, COO, MINNESOTA VIKINGS

"Paul Batz and Paul Hillen have proven that goodness pays. It is an essential part of winning in business and winning in life. This book paves the path for anyone interested in learning how to achieve great results by inspiring others and experiencing personal fulfillment along the journey as well as reaching the destination."

MEGAN REMARK, PRESIDENT AND CEO, REGIONS HOSPITAL

"Goodness pays. If you're a skeptic, this book was written for you. If you're a believer, the research and real-life evidence in this book will equip you to convince the skeptics around you. If you're a leader or aspiring to become one, you'll find both practical advice and inspiration in these pages. If you're in business, you should read this book!"

LORRI ANDERSON, HR EXECUTIVE, LOGIC PD

"*How Goodness Pays* is a long time coming: measuring the impact of human goodness in business. The collective ability of Batz and Hillen to cut things back to their bare essence and build them back up is impressive. The book itself is a precursor to a good business model."

RICK KUPCHELLA, FOUNDER AND CEO, I.E. NETWORK

"Why is common sense seldom common practice? Goodness pays—it's a core idea to living a good life. If you follow the insight in this book you will improve your business results, lead happier teams, and become a happier human being. How cool is that?"

DARIN LYNCH, FOUNDER AND CEO, IRISH TITAN

"*How Goodness Pays* proves Paul Batz is way ahead of the curve. His partnership with corporate executive Paul Hillen produced a must-read book for leaders who want to thrive in today's business culture."

STACEY STRATTON, PRESIDENT AND CEO, TRUE TALENT GROUP

"Paul Hillen and Paul Batz have written an insightful examination on how leading with goodness pays. Readers can gain knowledge on what it takes to lead with goodness and why something that seems like common sense is not common practice. This is a must read for anyone in leadership. The principles are clear and Batz and Hillen lay it out in a transparent easy to follow path."

NICKI VINCENT, EXECUTIVE DIRECTOR, ASSOCIATION FOR CORPORATE GROWTH

"I've learned and re-learned that my thinking needs to change in order to change behaviors, which is the foundation for any cultural shift. *How Goodness Pays* helps me continue to shift my thinking about my leadership shadow. I am looking forward to leveraging *How Goodness Pays* to amplify our ongoing culture journey to become a more mission-driven and values-based organization."

DAVE SPARKMAN, SENIOR VP, UNITEDHEALTH GROUP

"Paul Batz and team are on to something here! We have trained our managers and employees in the 'Seven Fs,' and they love it that their employer cares about them as whole people—not just employees. And it shows in their enthusiasm for the work!"

JODI HARPSTEAD, COO, LUTHERAN SOCIAL SERVICE OF MINNESOTA

"Obviously, in healthcare and the practice of neurosurgery, we believe in goodness. And yet, as physicians, we don't always know how to make it pay in the leadership part of our jobs. The advice in this book really works—it's been our path forward, and we are thriving."

PAUL CAMARATA, CHAIR, DEPARTMENT OF NEUROSURGERY, KU MEDICAL

"My leadership experience over the past ten years has been in big, global companies in both finance and technology areas of the business. Without a doubt, the ideas that Batz and Hillen share about goodness transcend cultural boundaries. And, in my experience, when our leaders lead with goodness, it really does pay. Thanks for sharing a great concept and a terrific book with the world."

JEFF AUGUSTIN, VP OF GLOBAL BUSINESS SERVICES, MERCK

"This leadership book contains actionable, evidence-based guidance for running an organization with a strong double-bottom line—that being profit and impact."

MATT NORMAN, PRESIDENT AND CEO, DALE CARNEGIE, NORTH CENTRAL US

"Paul Batz became my coach when my mentors gave me a second chance to lead my department out of a very difficult situation. This book distills the principles he helped me apply to support my colleagues' implementation of an amazing turnaround that has brought us closer to the cohesive, creative, thriving workplace to which we aspire. Read it, believe it, do it—it works!"

STEPHEN J. HAINES, FORMER HEAD, DEPARTMENT OF NEUROSURGERY, UNIVERSITY OF MINNESOTA

"There's no separation between good business and personal goodness. That's why *How Goodness Pays* is an important book for all business leaders."

JURRIAAN KAMP, FOUNDER-EDITOR *ODE MAGAZINE, THE OPTIMIST* AND *KAMP SOLUTIONS ACTIVATOR*

Good Leadership PRESS

About Good Leadership Press
Good Leadership Press publishes exciting books on positive leadership. The publisher and authors believe goodness pays, because goodness grows!

Each title features credible research, real stories of goodness at work in the world, practical leadership strategies, and coaching tools to help good leaders make goodness pay financially through their leadership.

To learn more about Good Leadership Press,
visit **goodleadership.com**

ISBN 13: 978-0-578-40260-4

Printed in the United States of America
First Printing: 2019
23 22 21 20 19   5 4 3 2 1

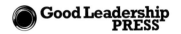

To order, visit **goodleadership.com**
Reseller discounts available.

Dedication

There are far too many individuals who contributed to this book over a four-year time horizon to appropriately recognize: the corporate brand group at Cargill, the Wealth Management team at U.S. Bank, SMS Research Advisors, employees of Good Leadership Enterprises, writing coaches, researchers, proofers, critical readers, coaches, designers… and the more than 16,000 guests of the Good Leadership Breakfast Series. All of these people have asked: "How can I help?" when they hear our mantra, goodness pays. We are grateful and energized by all of you. We trust you know who you are. And of course we need to thank our families who have supported us throughout our careers that made this book possible.

—Paul Batz and Paul Hillen, 2018

Contents

Foreword

By Richard H. Anderson,
President and Chief Executive Officer, Amtrak

I've often said effective leaders are those who come up with creative answers to hard problems. I believe the authors of *How Goodness Pays*, Paul Batz and Paul Hillen, have done just that. One of the hardest problems leaders face is figuring out how to effectively lead in ways in which everyone–owners, executives, employees and customers–can be successful. Which is why *How Goodness Pays* stands out as a leadership guide and captured my attention from its first few pages onward.

Readers will come away with a deeper understanding how everyday leadership practices, such as communicating with employees or building a compelling business plan, can be dramatically improved through plain old goodness. This may strike you as common sense–employing goodness in leadership–but as the authors note, common sense is not always common practice.

I can relate to the time, detailed early in this book, when Paul Hillen is told by Paul Batz (then his executive coach) that his leadership style at that time was like "a bag of hammers"–less effective and rubbing people the wrong way. I was once there too. Early in my career, I had a tendency to get impatient if things weren't going well

> *Unfortunately, when you lose your temper, it diminishes leadership effectiveness and hurts people.*

and lose my temper. Unfortunately, when you lose your temper, it diminishes leadership effectiveness and hurts people.

My CEO at the time took me aside and gave me some brief, invaluable instruction about the benefits of remaining patient and calm. I've never forgotten his advice. Today, I make a point to express my gratitude daily to the people who get the work done, as well as to our partners and customers. I regularly send hand-written thank-you notes.

At Delta Airlines, we needed to create a culture of treating customers in an exceptional way in all aspects of airline travel. We knew that for the most part, our airplanes and terminals were like all other airlines. So, it was important our employees knew we would set ourselves apart from competition with "The Delta Difference." While we did not necessarily call it "goodness" at the time, many of the goodness principles Batz and Hillen discuss in this book were important to our success.

As you read *How Goodness Pays*, I encourage you to do so with a pen or highlighter in-hand to note pages and paragraphs you think most applicable to your organization and style of leadership. I'd be surprised if you don't come away as I did, with multiple new ideas.

Leadership will always be difficult. By creatively thinking through a novel approach toward leadership–applying the principles of goodness–Paul Batz and Paul Hillen have provided a logical and easily accessible way of making leadership better–and softening that "bag of hammers."

Since 2017, Richard H. Anderson has served as President and Chief Executive Officer of Amtrak. Prior to Amtrak, he spent 25 years in the aviation industry, including serving as CEO of Delta Air Lines from 2007 to 2016 and as Executive Director of the airline's Board of Directors.

Introduction:
How Goodness Pays

By Paul Hillen
Former Chief Marketing Officer at Cargill
Current President and COO at Revier Brand Group, LLC at Revier
Cattle Company

In the fall of 2004, my faith in myself as a leader was shaken to the core. Over 15 successful years in sales, marketing, and general management at Procter & Gamble (P&G), and an additional two years at Cargill, I always received positive feedback on my leadership style and had achieved good business results. After joining Cargill, I spent two years thinking I was taking the company's food ingredient team in a bold and transformative new direction–until I got feedback in a leadership development program that some peers and members of my team didn't trust me.

It really hit me hard, until I understood it more. It wasn't that these people thought I was devious or dishonest. Instead, their lack of trust was linked to their perceptions of my motives. They questioned whether my efforts were in their best interests or mine. In their eyes, my tight meeting agendas and well-thought-out strategy and goals documents were self-serving because they were created in isolation, without any of their input. While I thought I was being prepared and "buttoned-up" by coming to meetings with rigorous, carefully considered plans, my team thought my leadership style was insincere. No one believed I cared about them as people–only as worker bees there to help me look good.

In short, many on my team at Cargill said I was only looking out for myself. I thought I was doing what was best for the company. I was simply using the skills and discipline I had been taught at P&G where that leadership style was expected and rewarded as proactive and efficient. However, at Cargill it was seen as self-focused. After I received this feedback, I spent the next two weeks stewing, wondering if Cargill was the right place for me.

Keen Insight from a Good Leader

While I was still stewing about my stinging feedback, my 12-year-old son's leg was shattered during a baseball game when a player slid into him at home plate, while he was playing catcher.

Two weeks after my son's accident, I was leaving a meeting at the executive offices of Cargill when I encountered our CEO, Greg Page. I was walking down the stairway, and he was racing upward, obviously not wanting to be late for his next meeting. We passed each other, and both quickly said hello. As I took about three more steps, I heard him call my name.

"Hey Paul!" he shouted. "How's your son?"

I just kept walking down the stairs and said "Greg, don't worry, you look late for your meeting!" After all, this was the CEO of a $100+ billion, 150,000-employee international corporation. I wrongly assumed that for our CEO, business came way before concerns over an employee's son's broken leg. But I was wrong.

Page stopped, and said "No, Paul…" He began walking down the stairs, back toward me. "I heard his injury was awful." He stopped in the middle of the staircase. "How is he doing?"

That was the beginning of my "aha" moment. Page stopped when he was already clearly late for something important to show care and concern for me. He spent about five minutes asking about my son, my family...and about how I was doing at Cargill. CEOs get to choose how they spend their time during the day, and he chose to be late for something to learn more about me. Those five minutes were more meaningful to me than the entire two prior years that I had spent at Cargill. As Page sprinted back up the stairs, I thought "Wow, that was great of him to take the time." I already respected Page as a leader, but that interaction really cemented in my mind his leadership abilities. In those relatively few minutes, he demonstrated to me a lifetime learning opportunity precisely when I needed it most—the powerfully positive impact of knowing that a leader truly cares.

Years later, I've amended my conclusion; not only do leaders like Page demonstrate the positive impact of caring about people, they demonstrate the impact of how goodness pays in leadership. From that day forward, I changed my approach. I invested in the lives of the people around me and my business results followed. And I did it with goodness.

> *From that day forward, I changed my approach. I invested in the lives of the people around me and my business results followed. And I did it with goodness.*

Goodness Defined

The word "goodness" is rarely heard in the lexicon of business. It's usually seen as a secondary focus used for branding or corporate social responsibility messaging. Many leaders—I used to be one of them—perceive goodness as a soft or fluffy behavior not really important in day-to-day business activity. Or some think of goodness only as a religious or spiritual term, which is not easily measured. Yet other leaders believe goodness, as an underlying motivator, can be easily exploited by fierce competitive forces. This book was written to dispel all of those beliefs and prove how goodness pays.

I've learned over time that goodness in leadership is an others-focused approach that creates and sustains momentum, even in the face of great challenges. **Goodness in business is when people** *thrive together* **in a culture of encouragement, accountability, and positive teamwork.** Good leadership results in magnetism that creates followership and attracts and retains the best employees.

Softening a "Bag of Hammers"

I met Paul Batz when he was assigned as my executive coach as part of a Cargill leadership development program called *Future Focused Leaders.* Paul met with me a couple of times, read my feedback report that said some of my team members didn't trust me, and called my leadership style a "bag of hammers." He pointed out that my style works great if I'm in a culture that values individual leadership, but it would not work where personal relationships were important. He said to be successful as an enterprise leader at Cargill or similar organizations, I had to change my approach to build trust.

My original hard, fast, and direct leadership style was learned behavior growing up as the youngest of seven kids in a tough-love family, and my style was rewarded early in my career. I thrived in P&G's results-only, up-or-out culture. However, after the feedback at Cargill and the advice from my coach, I softened my approach, and that was a good thing. I've always cared deeply about getting results in my work, but I learned to ask myself the question *"At what cost to others?"* By learning to care more about the people who work for me, the work I care so much about gets done better, faster and cheaper–and everyone thrives together. I learned that lesson from Greg Page, and from Paul Batz' mantra ringing in my ears: **Goodness Pays.**

> *By learning to care more about the people who work for me, the work I care so much about gets done better, faster and cheaper–and everyone thrives together.*

A Good Business Investment

I believe *How Goodness Pays* is ***the one book*** every leader, business owner, executive and aspiring CEO needs to read in order to achieve consistent business success. I'm still a direct leader, with a short attention span, and a glass-half-empty orientation. I prefer making decisions with facts and data over soft and squishy information. I also believe the most important business results are *financial.* That's why I believe this book is so important, because our data shows how goodness pays financially for leaders and for their organizations. I would love to see every business school and corporate training program teach goodness as a motivating force for leadership.

CHAPTER 1
"What Are You, an F'n Do-Gooder?"

I received an e-mail that hardened my resolve to prove how goodness pays.

The subject line simply said: "COMMENT."

The body of the email said: "What are you, an F'n Do-Gooder?" That was it.

The sender's name was unfamiliar. I replied back and asked "What do you mean?" All that came back was an AOL bounceback message–a dead end. The hollow exchange sparked a self-talk debate inside my head:

> *"Am I an F'n Do-Gooder? Probably. Why does that feel weird to say?*
> *If not, then why not? Is that a good thing, or a bad thing?*
> *If I'm not an F'n Do-Gooder, does that make me an F'n Do-Badder?*
> *That just sounds bad."*

That was eight years ago. Despite this type of resistance, my firm, Good Leadership Enterprises, stayed on message and built a thriving leadership development business through coaching, writing, and speaking about how goodness pays for our clients.

The word "goodness" applied to leadership creates a polarizing response in most people–hardly anyone is neutral on this term. Skeptics, like Paul Hillen, at first dismiss the concept of goodness in leadership as too soft, weak, or religious. But the vast majority of successful leaders endorse goodness as a motivator for their ongoing business success. They just may not call it goodness, or even realize they are doing it.

> Our Definition: **Goodness in business is when people *thrive together* in a culture of encouragement, accountability, and positive teamwork.** Goodness is an others-focused approach that creates and sustains business momentum, even in uncertain or difficult business environments.

This book is an unapologetic statement, supported by data, to show *how* goodness pays in business.

Making the Case: How Does Goodness Pay?

For more than eight years, we have been collecting input through audience response technology in a variety of forums–meetings, retreats, and conventions–about goodness as a catalyst for business success. What have we learned? *Four out of five* leaders surveyed believe goodness pays in leadership and business. And yet only *two out of five* of those same leaders are happy with the consistency of their financial results–they believe that goodness pays but they don't know how to make it pay in business profits. This book, *How Goodness Pays*, closes that gap by specifically teaching those who believe that goodness pays how to achieve consistently positive financial results following goodness practices.

Inspiration from Grandma

This project was inspired by a conversation I had during the United States debt-ceiling crisis, with Richard Davis, who at the time was CEO of U.S. Bank, one of the nation's ten largest banks. "I'm inclined to support this project because of what I call the 'grandmother clause,'" Davis explained. Like all of the other major bank CEOs at the time, he was feeling smothered by scrutiny from the White House, Congress, and business media.

Davis credits the grandmother clause as one of the reasons that U.S. Bank avoided the self-inflicted missteps of similar banks that were deemed "too big to fail." He explained his meaning of the grandmother clause: "I've always asked our bankers to run their ideas and our products through an ethically-narrow filter: *Would we sell this to our grandmothers?*" Davis said. That fundamental belief system instilled in the company's bankers a more risk-averse set of behaviors that kept U.S. Bank on a more even-keeled, prosperous path, while peer companies faltered due to offering potentially ethically-questionable products.

U.S. Bank not only emerged relatively unscathed by the financial crisis and public mistrust of large banking institutions, but quickly began accelerating as the economy improved. Over Davis' 11 years as CEO, the financial performance of U.S. Bank exceeded its peer group, as reported by *The Wall Street Journal*.

Davis' encouragement to me was motivating and exceptionally credible. In 2010, *American Banker* chose Davis as "Banker of the Year" and the *Twin Cities Business Journal* designated him "Executive of the Year." In 2011, he received the Hendrickson Medal for Ethical Leadership. And two years after our breakfast meeting, U.S. Bank earned the 2015 World's Most Ethical Company award from the Ethisphere Institute.

When Davis said "You are doing important work," he validated my identity as an "F'n Do-Gooder," and motivated me to prove how goodness pays.

Beliefs Affect Results

The late management guru Peter Drucker taught in business school "*The purpose of a business is to create and keep a customer.*" If you believe that, then the purpose of a business leader is to create and keep customers in ways that generate consistently positive financial results. It's what owners and shareholders expect in both public and private organizations.

So that begs the question: As a business leader, are you regularly happy with the consistency of *your* financial results?

If you said "no," you should know that you are not alone. Earlier in this chapter, I shared how only two out of five–just 40%– of business leaders we surveyed over the past eight years reported that they were happy with the consistency of the financial performance of their organizations. That's an eye-opening statistic.

We believe the best way for businesses to achieve consistently positive financial performance is to start with the fundamental belief: **Goodness Pays**. What that really means is we have to push back the temptation to use short-term thinking to hit our financial goals. I don't believe the opposite of goodness is *badness, evil* or *greed*. Rather, it's the feeling that we *have to do things* in the short term that we know in the back of our minds will hurt the business in the long term.

> *I don't believe the opposite of goodness is badness, evil or greed.*

Most leaders really do intend to do the right thing for employees, customers, and the business. But the resistance that builds up from self-justified, short-term decisions, ultimately becomes the opposite of goodness.

In the pages that follow, we will answer the "How does goodness pay?" question with data and stories about how leading with goodness can enable your business to:

- Recruit and retain the best employees

- Magnetically attract and keep the best customers

- Deliver consistently positive financial results

While the skeptics might pause here, the rest of us ask: "Isn't leading with goodness a common sense thing to do?" The answer is, of course it is! But as we all know from experience; common sense is not always common practice. Chapters 4-8 explain five common sense, goodness-based factors that are linked to consistently positive financial results. We call them the Five Goodness Pays Factors:

 Compelling business plan (Chapter 4)
Prepare a business plan that creates genuine employee engagement and followership.

 Belief that profits are healthy for all (Chapter 5)
Build commitment to the idea that profits are beneficial for everyone in the business–employees, executives, and owners.

 Team-based culture (Chapter 6)
Create a culture that rewards a "we is greater than me" approach in which multiple people are accountable and rewarded for delivering on important promises.

 Timely and transparent decision-making (Chapter 7)
Gain employee respect by making decisions in a timely fashion and by being accountable for the behaviors and results that come from those decisions.

Magnetic ethics (Chapter 8)
Attract good people by role modeling what is and what is not acceptable.

If a skeptical "bag of hammers" leader like Paul Hillen can learn to lead with goodness, then any leader has that same potential. Within a few years of his coaching experience, Hillen won coveted 100 Most Talented Global Marketing Leaders awards in 2014 and 2016 from the World Marketing Congress, and he was chosen by his peers as a Top CMO by the CMO Club in 2015. But most importantly, Hillen earned the following LinkedIn endorsement from a direct report, showcasing the type of personal relationship that was previously missing in his leadership:

> I've had the good fortune to work with many talented leaders during my career, but I don't think there is one leader I've learned so much from in such a short period of time as I have from Paul Hillen. Paul is an exceptional marketer, with a disciplined approach, customer-centric focus, and unmatched analytical expertise. Paul has the unique talent of being both extremely creative yet strategically adept. He is particularly skilled at articulating complex subjects and processes in an easy-to-understand and practical manner. Paul expertly navigates various relationships including senior executives, agencies, global colleagues, and management teams. Paul leads by example, demonstrating unique insights, dynamic execution, and always pushing his peers and team to accomplish what seems impossible while exceeding all expectations.

Bottom-line, this is a book for leaders of businesses of all types and sizes–small, mid-sized, and large–who are seeking a better, more sustainable way to lead their organizations to solid, consistent business success.

Onward, because *Goodness Pays*!

The Skeptic's Shift

By Paul Hillen

In my 32-year career, I've come to believe the most common factor in bad leadership behavior is fear. While fear is the greatest motivator of all human emotions, it is only short-term. It does not get healthy, long-term results for companies, employees, or owners. When people are afraid to make decisions and afraid they might lose, they probably **will** lose. Have you ever had success being afraid most of the time?

As my wife and I were preparing to move our family from Cincinnati to Houston where I would manage a planned joint venture between P&G and Coca Cola, I was recruited by Cargill, an agribusiness company, to move to Minneapolis and help develop a new food strategy. I had spent 15 years at P&G working amid a competitive, high-pressure culture. Not only was there constant pressure at the corporate level to deliver quarterly expectations for Wall Street; at my level, in brand management, it was an up-or-out environment. If you did not meet sales expectations contributing to earnings, you were sent packing and replaced. Looking back at my time at P&G, I now realize fear was my dominant emotion.

In this high-pressure environment, I was too busy to let the concept of goodness get in the way of delivering business results. Who had time for the "fluffy, soft stuff" of goodness? We were there to do a job at a very high level and if we did not deliver, they'd find someone else to do it. My thinking then was "goodness? What does that have to do with delivering business results?"

In retrospect, related to goodness, I now realize it wasn't about what I did, but rather what I didn't do. I didn't take the time to recognize people for their work. I didn't compliment others very often. I didn't point out the positives in our workplace. There wasn't time, or so I thought. It was all about doing things better. It led me to constantly point out to my direct reports what could be done better, and not spend time with them discussing what they were doing well.

At P&G, I believed goodness *got in the way* of drive; however, I came to realize that goodness *provides* the drive. The shift came when I was meeting with Greg Page, then our CEO at Cargill. He said to me that people knew I was trying to take them in the right direction, but they did not always want to follow. He said, "People need to follow *because* of you, not in *spite* of you." His point was that I needed to bring them along with me by involving them early, inspiring them with what was possible, and encouraging them to persevere to get there.

At the time, I did not interpret Greg's advice as "goodness," but it certainly was. His advice was consistent with promoting fairness by involving people early in the process, and spreading positivity by showing them what was possible with their involvement. I don't believe I was managing out of fear, but I clearly wasn't managing through positivity and rewarding excellence. Once I made that shift, my effectiveness improved, the speed of results increased, and the feedback I got was much better. People were now following *because* of me.

CHAPTER 2
The "Why?" Behind the Concept of Goodness Pays

"Good leaders thrive because they enjoy what they do. They're ful-filled because people flock to good leaders. It's about positivity, and the idea of 'the more you give, the more you receive.' If you live a life of goodness, you will be richly rewarded."

Colleen Needles Steward, CEO at Tremendous! Entertainment

Articulating the "why" behind goodness pays relies on both ancient wisdom and modern research. The short answer to the question *"Why does goodness pay in leadership?"* is that what we give out to others comes back to us. It's basic human behavior. But that only makes sense to zealots who don't need to see a good argument to believe a good concept. There are three fundamental reasons why goodness pays, beyond basic human behavior:

1. People are significantly more likely to help rather than hurt a fellow human-it's the fundamental reason why people live and work together. Most people are happier and more productive when they help each other.

2. People react positively to goodness, because most information channels today are dominated by "dark noise"-practically constant negative news coverage-which is spread at the speed of light. The volume of

dark noise gives some people the false impression that stories of people getting hurt vastly outnumber the acts of excellence, generosity, fairness, and positivity associated with goodness.

3 The speed of change in every part of our lives continues to accelerate. It's difficult because most people are threatened by the fear of the unknown associated with change. Neuroscience research confirms that we crave leaders who are warm, encouraging, and who radiate goodness–that's *why* goodness pays.

Helping is Natural, Hurting is Learned

It's worth repeating that the definition of goodness involves the idea that people *thrive together.* Human society is based on cooperation, and our survival as a species has been directly linked to helping each other. Anthropologists have confirmed that long ago, we simply wouldn't have survived threats of weather, famine, and aggression by animals or enemies if we didn't have the instinct to help each other.

Research organizations like Alberta Health Services and the University of London have published results from studies supporting the idea that working in groups and helping each other through problems can significantly raise collective levels of achievement, reinforcing the idea that helping others helps ourselves. Their studies indicate that we are born with an innate desire to help others.

In his book, *Why We Cooperate*, developmental psychologist Dr. Michael Tomasello details how infants intuitively help others, based on studying the behavior of 12- to 18-month-old infants. "Children are altruistic by nature," he writes. "Most social norms are about being nice to other people, so children learn social norms to help each other because they want to be a part of a group."

Tomasello observed that when toddlers see an unrelated adult whose hands are full and who needs assistance opening a door or picking up a dropped clothespin, they will immediately help. The behaviors are deemed to be innate because they show up before the polite rules of behavior are taught by parents.

Tomasello's research also sheds light on how we learn to hurt others, through what psychologists call the law of reciprocity. It's our deep-rooted psychological urge to do something good for those who have done something good for us, and vice-versa. Researchers have found that people who feel helped by another often repay their gratitude with even greater amounts of kindness and cooperation than they originally received. Conversely, perceived self-serving behavior by others is frequently met with higher-than-expected levels of anger and retribution.

In other words, the law of reciprocity works like this: If you do "good" to me, I will return that good to you, and I might even do more for you than you did for me. However, if you do "bad" to me, I will likely return that behavior in ways that are worse than I think you did to me.

Reciprocity in Business

Charles Antis, CEO at Antis Roofing & Waterproofing in Irvine, California, learned a powerful lesson about goodness starting in 2009, during a global recession. Like many business owners and leaders, Antis, for years, took his employees for granted. "When I first started my business in 1989, I didn't care about my employees as much as I do today," Antis admitted.

But that all changed as Antis' business–like others in the construction industry–suffered a steep, recession-driven sales downturn. Antis watched as many of his industry peers laid off their workers, wondering if he might need to follow suit. But he didn't want to lose the faith and loyalty of the craftspeople he had so carefully recruited and trained over the years. So instead of laying off his experienced roofers, Antis committed his company to an aggressive pro bono strategy to keep his employees engaged with meaningful work.

In consultation with local community leaders, Antis decided that his best immediate business strategy was to donate all of the roofing materials and labor for every Habitat for Humanity home being built in Orange County, an area with a population of more than 3 million. The strategy paid immediate results. Not only did this move help Antis retain his best workers, the visibility of this huge commitment also created a big upswing in the company's roofing business as the economy gradually improved.

More than a decade later, Antis Roofing continues to contribute roofs for every Habitat for Humanity home in Orange County, and is now one of the county's fastest-growing and largest roofing companies, focusing on serving homeowners' associations and multi-tenant communities. The company's generosity has been publicly noticed. In 2017, the company swept the National Roofing Contractors Association annual awards, winning the Community Involvement Award, the MVP Award, and the Best of the Best Award.

Antis learned that treating his employees better taught him how to be a better leader. "I knew we needed to show our employees we cared about them, or they wouldn't return to us when sales increased," he said. "So, we turned our focus outward, keeping everyone busy by being socially responsible in our community. That goodness paid for us in so many ways. But first and foremost, we saw the importance of helping our employees during a tough time, so they would return that same level of effort in helping us grow."

Today, Antis Roofing spends significantly more time and money than other roofing companies listening to employees' needs and investing in training to improve their personal and professional skills. As a result, the company's turnover went down, quality and productivity went up, and customers kept returning because of the company's excellent work. "The success of our entire enterprise comes from our commitment to help each other–from the CEO to the newest employee–and out into our community," Antis said. "That's what I call goodness."

Employee Wellness Leads to Goodness Payoff

What Antis discovered about employee loyalty and productivity through the steps he took as a small business owner–thinking first about his employees' personal and professional interests–is what many larger companies think of as employee wellness. For the same reasons that Antis adopted an employee-centric approach, the corporate employee wellness industry has increased in importance, because the best employers want to retain the best employees and they want those employees to be happy and healthy.

Mary Kruse, CEO at HealthSource Solutions located in Hopkins, Minnesota, whose firm consults with companies on how to increase the bottom-line benefits associated with employee wellness, explains how companies like hers benefit their clients: "Wellness research over the past decade has shown that we need to move past the focus on the physical, and include other areas such as financial, social, and emotional well-being. Employees who feel valued and supported are more productive, have lower turnover, manage stress better, and are more proactive in managing their health. We also know that the well-being of the employees is a direct extension of how invested leadership is in walking the talk. Behavior change is hard. Leaders who model positivity, empathy, and encouragement have the greatest results in shifting their corporate culture."

Companies that invest in wellness or well-being programs know it's more than just changing an individual behavior. It's about creating a culture with an unmistakable "we care about you" message. Its where small steps do make a difference–making the healthy choice the easy choice, people always supersede projects, and fun is an acceptable stress reliver. It's about building a culture that nurtures daily health habits such as walking meetings, fresh fruit, and social breaks. It's building expectation (through policy) that PTO is to be used and that working overtime is not the norm. Goodness pays when employees believe you have their best interests at heart.

Kruse also noted that with a tight labor market and the increasing challenge of recruiting top talent, it's imperative that companies treat employees well and build their culture around appreciation and value. She said: "Treating employees as your most valued asset will provide a direct return on investment through customer service, quality of work, and problem solving. Do you frequent a restaurant where the server is rude? Of course not! The places that get your business treat their employees well, so they treat you well. It's the baseline of goodness at work."

Building on Cornerstones

According to Kruse and many others, treating your employees well is foundational for business success. Our research for this book identified the four fundamental, goodness-related values necessary for achieving that kind of positive workplace dynamic. We call them the *Cornerstones of Goodness*:

- **Rewarding excellence**

- **Living generously**

- **Promoting fairness**

- **Spreading positivity**

Each of these Cornerstones, when seen and felt throughout the workplace, contribute to a positive, others-centric culture in which everyone–owners, leaders, employees, and customers–wins. Here's how:

Rewarding excellence: Culture is formed by what gets rewarded. The top players in any organization expect to be rewarded for producing excellence. Conversely, employees quickly see when leaders allow others to cut corners or look the other way when quality slips.

Living generously: Teams form more quickly and people give their best effort to leaders who are generous in sharing their time, thoughts, energy, and resources in developing the business and its employees.

Promoting fairness: Fairness becomes a cultural norm when leaders treat all employees with the same level of respect, regardless of role or title. Good leaders make timely and transparent decisions and provide opportunities for everyone to grow their careers.

Spreading positivity: Organizations thrive when their leaders can consistently provide a positive environment for their employees, who, in turn, feed on and multiply that positivity. In our interviews, literature reviews, and surveys conducted for this book, the most frequently used word related to goodness was "positivity."

Overcoming Dark Noise

Of the four Cornerstones, spreading positivity is the most powerful, because, in the context of a world filled with bad news, we are magnetically drawn to people who help us feel good about ourselves and help us stay positive. Why is this so important?

Negative experiences can take an even heavier weight on our moods because our daily lives are often dominated by what could be called "dark noise." As the term implies, dark noise is an overexposure to negative news stories about people suffering through such things as natural disasters, accidents, diseases, terrorists, corporate and political misbehaviors, and atrocious crimes against humanity. A dark noise day typically begins with a TV or radio on in the background as you're making breakfast, updating you on all sorts of local, national, and international calamities. Then, your phone buzzes with news updates, which get replayed every 20 minutes over the car radio or on cable news.

Dark noise is an overexposure to negative news stories about people suffering.

The dark noise phenomena happens because we're living in an era of the 24-hour news cycle in which news, opinions, rumors, and misinformation move into our lives instantaneously and repetitively. We want to stay informed about what's happening on the global and local levels of our society. But, unfortunately, it seems as if most forms of media are now dominated by grindingly harsh news.

No wonder 60% of 3,440 Americans surveyed in 2017 considered the state of our national affairs to be at "the lowest point in our nation's history that they can remember," as reported by Fortune. com. According to the magazine *The Week*, people said that the main sources of darkness in their lives are a distrust of government, media negativity, crime, terrorism, and international conflicts.

Without hearing a broader perspective, it would be easy for news consumers to conclude that the entire world is dominated by people hurting–or at least being unkind to–each other on an ongoing basis. It's not true, but it's stressful to consume the negative news stream every day.

Indicative of the dark noise phenomena, the American Psychological Association (APA) in 2017 identified a disturbing trend reflective of the collective state of our nation's mental health. The APA's "Stress in America" survey revealed "fear and anxiety about politics and the future of the country are a significant source of stress for nearly two-thirds of adults in the United States." This aligns with what we found in our research for this book–that what employees seek the most today in the workplace, perhaps as a counterbalance to the dark noise, is a sense of positivity from their employers.

Strategies to Break through the Darkness

To counteract the effects of dark noise, many people–perhaps even you–are responding with at least one of two strategies. First, by canceling your news subscriptions, turning off the cable news channels, and avoiding talk radio, reducing your exposure to the news. It's no coincidence that in early 2018, Life Time Fitness, one of the nation's largest health club chains, removed all 24-hour news channels from the massive flat-screen televisions in the common areas at its fitness centers. The reason? A growing number of Life Time clients felt that being exposed to these channels was inconsistent with having a healthy lifestyle.

The second response to the era of dark noise is more compelling for business leaders–employees at all levels are seeking far more meaning and positivity in their work. When employees feel goodness at work, they develop a more positive mood about their lives–as opposed to being sent into a veritable tailspin, due to being regularly exposed to negativity about matters they cannot control.

Consider what a female executive shared with me: "My father went into hospice this week. My spouse is unemployed and very bitter. Our teenage son is confused and acting out–he has been suspended from school because of truancy. This morning, I turned off the radio because there was news of yet another mass shooting, and I just couldn't handle any more darkness."

She continued: "The one thing right now in my life that makes me feel good about myself is going to work." As she spoke, her body language became more confident and energetic. "At work, I have great colleagues. I like the fact that my CEO gives me control over the work on my desk. And I love the feeling of being successful, accomplishing meaningful things for customers I adore, and producing results with my team that make us all proud. My work is what helps me be the best person I can be."

What a great gift for her to share that insight! A positive, encouraging workplace creates focus on producing results that people can be proud of. That's why the leaders we interviewed for this book consistently see goodness as not just a "feel-good" response, but rather a business strategy to meet the financial expectations of their stakeholders.

Good Leaders Thrive, Bad Leaders Survive

Lynn Casey, Chair at Padilla, has a first-hand perspective about the positive impact of goodness in leadership. Casey's firm is widely recognized as one of the world's most successful mid-sized public relations/communications firms. She counsels leaders whose reputations are formed in the court of public opinion. "From what I've seen, good leaders thrive and bad leaders just survive," she observed. "And that goes for their firms as well. Goodness in leadership is not easy. When good leaders thrive, they take the burden on themselves. The bad leaders put the burdens on the employees. And that emanates outward really fast in ways that can hurt a lot of people."

Consider, for example, Berkshire Hathaway CEO Warren Buffet. Lauded as an astute investor and the world's second-richest man, Buffet successfully leads nearly 400,000 employees in his companies through a values-based, hands-off approach that gives individual company leaders wide leeway in their decision-making and incents them like owners. "We count very heavily on principles of behavior rather than loads of rules," Buffet shared at an annual shareholders meeting, as he stressed the importance of employees acting with integrity, working with focus, and always learning.

By contrast, there are leaders, such as the late hotelier Leona Helmsley, so tyrannical to her employees that she earned the nickname "The Queen of Mean." Famous attorney Alan Dershowitz recalled that, during breakfast with Helmsley at one of her hotels, a waiter brought him a cup of tea with a small bit of water on the saucer. Helmsley grabbed the cup and saucer, shattered them on the floor, then told the waiter: "Now clean it up and beg for your job."

The real cost of letting dark noise and negativity dominate our psyche is a loss of hope.

The real cost of letting dark noise and negativity dominate our psyche is a loss of hope. Businesses cannot thrive without employees who have hope. The problem is, if people at work today need to feel hope and optimism from their leaders, we have a lot of work to do. According to research from Georgetown University, nearly two-thirds of Americans report they were bullied at work in 2016, which is up from nearly half in 1998. That means more than half of the workers in America claim to have been "treated rudely at least once a month" by bosses or co-workers in the past year, according to the study. This recurring cycle of belittling behavior eats away at hope and certainly does not spread positivity.

Greg Page, retired CEO and Chair at Cargill, went even deeper on the power of preserving hope in leadership. Page predicts that in the future, goodness will be the minimum ante for leadership success. "In the face of all the noise, I think leaders going forward are going to have to be self-controlled and self-disciplined to cut through the confusion, and to pay attention to what really matters so that they can stay optimistic," he explained. "Because if you're not relentlessly determined and genuinely optimistic, the people around you won't have much hope."

Neuroscience Supports the Power of Goodness

We've all heard the statement "the only constant is change." The faster things change, the more relevant that mindset becomes. Graeme Wood, a national correspondent for *The Atlantic*, famously wrote in 2009 "Change has never happened this fast before, and it will never be this slow again." If Wood's assertion is true–and I believe it is–it's a quote that will never go out of date.

It's relevant because most people resist change. Some people become subversive and destructive resistors. For business leaders, it means we need to constantly prepare people for change to avoid being overtaken by negativity.

Goodness helps leaders focus their people's attention on aspirational "what's possible?" thinking in times of disruptive change. The plethora of neuroscience research cited today in newspapers, magazines, and blogs points to how our brains are literally addicted to the chemicals that are emitted when new insights are formed by aspirational thinking about the future. The longer leaders let people look backwards, dwelling on what they believe to be the "problem" that led to the change, the less likely they will be able to produce the positive insights needed to break out of resistance.

Some of the groundbreaking research in this field was shared in the 2006 *Booz & Company* article "The Neuroscience of Leadership." Researchers David Rock and Michael Schwartz explained how neuroscience demonstrates that positive leadership helps shape the dominant pathways in the brain. Taking into account the physiological nature of the brain, experiments involving brain chemistry show that people are predisposed to resist some forms of leadership and to accept others.

In the simplest of terms, neuroscientists have confirmed that our brains fire a rapid response to either fight or flee from bullying styles–those which we perceive to threaten our self-interests. Instead, our brains crave relationship styles that are warm, encouraging, and perceived as positive to our self-interests.

The amygdala is the part of the brain which is significantly involved in aggression–the fight or flight response. A leadership style which creates chronic stress or trauma makes employees' amygdala significantly more excitable, increasing the likelihood that these employees will be increasingly aggressive toward one another.

Constant stress also puts strain on our brains' frontal cortices, which control emotions, impulses, and judgment. So, aggressive leadership styles cause poorer decision-making and unpredictable behaviors. But most significantly, recent discoveries have proven that when we are stressed at work, we become less compassionate and less empathetic. It therefore sets off a negative ripple effect that can really hurt your business. If employees feel stress and anxiety in their workplace, the risk is that they will "let off steam" by passing along their fear and angst to your customers. Can you afford that risk to your customer base?

The Journal of Psychosomatic Medicine published a report in 2016 called "The Neurobiology of Giving Versus Receiving Support: The Role of Stress-Related and Social Reward-Related Neural Activity." It's a heavy title for an insightful article about the ways in which helping others benefits the chemistry of our brains. In short, the happy chemicals in the brain respond significantly more when we demonstrate selflessness and help others, as opposed to behaving with "meanness and selfishness." There is also evidence from many other studies to show how expressing generosity and gratitude can create an upward spiral of well-being and positive brain health.

This research highlights what we already know intuitively-that aggressive leadership styles generate more "dark noise" at work. Goodness works better because people are genetically predisposed to environments in which they feel personally valued and believe that they can thrive by working together.

In sum, this is not a call for soft and squishy leadership in which everyone gets a participation trophy regardless of outcomes. It's about feeding our neuroscientific need to *help each other win*-both personally and professionally.

Harder to Earn Trust Today–But Even More Important

Perhaps the best way to summarize "why" goodness pays is to show how goodness correlates with trust, an increasingly valued commodity in business. The global public relations and communications firm, Edelman, created the Edelman Trust Barometer several years ago in order to measure the trust people felt about businesses and governments. The 2017 Edelman survey found that trust is in crisis throughout the world. The global population's trust in four key institutions–business, government, non-government organizations, and the media–had all declined broadly.

The following year, the 2018 Edelman Trust Barometer survey reinforced this new public sense of distrust in previously respected institutions. From the report: "For the first time, media is the least trusted institution globally. In 22 of the 28 countries surveyed it is now distrusted. In fact, 63% of respondents said they do not know how to tell good journalism from rumor or falsehoods, or whether or not a piece of news was produced by a respected media organization. The lack of faith in media has also led to an inability to identify the truth (59%), trust government leaders (56%), and trust business (42%)."

Edelman's findings also support our assertion that good work heals. "Business is now expected to be an agent of change. The employer is the new safe house in global governance, with 72% of respondents saying they trust their own company. And 64% believe a company can take actions that both increase profits and improve economic and social conditions in the community where it operates."

It's no wonder that customers and employees who are losing faith in the general media have become broadcast journalists on their own, using nothing more than smartphones or computers to spread their messages. Those who feel unfairly treated by a business, whether a customer or employee, are now broadcasting their angst on social media sites, in full view of the public and the mainstream media, with the power to amplify such messages. For proof, just ask former Uber founder and CEO Travis Kalanick what happened to his future as CEO after he berated his Uber driver on camera. The driver became a whistle-blower journalist by posting his own point-of-view video, which was eventually viewed by millions. This event directly contributed to Kalanick's ousting as CEO, despite his financial successes and innovator credentials with Uber.

Goodness Helps with International Business

As businesses expand their services and customer bases across international borders, goodness can add exponential value. Acts of goodness transcend ethnic, cultural, and language barriers forging greater mutual trust. Leaders who believe goodness pays operate with a level of transparency and good intentions that others can sense and act upon, even when language is a barrier. As Stephen Covey wrote in his best-selling book, *The Speed of Trust:* "The difference between a high- and low-trust relationship is palpable."

Building trust in international business is important because of the inherent, trust-associated barriers that exist when transacting business with people from other countries. Think how often you've heard a global business executive say something like "We can't do business in (Country X) because they're so tough to work with." Or "If only our sales prospects in (Country Y) could understand us better, we could get better traction."

> *Leaders who believe goodness pays operate with a level of transparency and good intentions that others can sense and act upon, even when language is a barrier.*

According to Covey, a strong business case can be made for the importance of goodness in international business relationships, as trust directly impacts speed and cost. When trust is high, speed increases and costs go down; when trust is low, speed decreases and costs go up. Covey cites the trust-related example of pre- and post-9/11 airport security. Prior to 9/11, a ticketed passenger could speedily board any plane. After 9/11, as we all know, it takes longer for passengers to pass through airport security and board a plane and it's also more expensive, due to the scrutiny and cost of the added security measures.

In international business, low trust can come with the territory–but it doesn't need to. "Authenticity gives leaders a 'multiplier effect' when communicating with people in places where English is not their primary language," said Dr. Katherine Holt. Her firm, Global Coach, LLC, is a global leadership development firm. As such, Holt has keen insights into the type of leadership required to achieve international business success–starting with the ability of leaders to authentically connect with those from other countries, and to build a greater sense of trust.

"Much of the world does business in English as the unifying language, but English has a lot of slang, and double-negative word choices that make understanding through words alone difficult," Holt said. "In those moments of difficulty, when the words are confusing, that's when things like sincerity and authenticity, which are associated with goodness, actually say more than words."

By demonstrating your goodness, in both word and deed, you can build trust faster which more effectively expands your international business opportunities. The outcome? Better business results, greater customer loyalty, and increased likelihood your customers will refer you to others. That's how goodness pays!

The Skeptic's Shift
From the Golden Rule to the Platinum Rule

By Paul Hillen

One of the problems I faced as a leader for the first 20 years of my career is that I followed the Golden Rule–treat others the way *you* want to be treated. Yes, that's right, it was a problem. I spent years treating people the way *I* wanted to be treated. The problem was, I didn't expect to be treated in ways that recognized excellence or radiated positivity–key elements of goodness.

I thought telling my co-workers about my weekend, or my personal life was a waste of time. So, I didn't ask my co-workers about their weekends or their personal lives. We were there to drive the business, and family time was for non-work hours.

Since I started working with Paul Batz as my coach, I've rewritten my life rule from the Golden Rule to the Platinum Rule–treat others how *they* want to be treated. I first read about it in the book aptly called *The Platinum Rule* by Tony Alessandra and

Michael J. O'Connor. As a professional marketer, I know the importance of understanding the needs of others. That's the essence of the Platinum Rule.

Applying the Platinum Rule changed my professional and personal life because I learned to be others-focused and to understand what others care about and need for their own success. I started managing *individuals* instead of the *organization*. It changed how I interacted with and motivated others.

It should be no surprise that once I began employing the Platinum Rule, my business goals became easier to achieve. The more people learned that I cared about them, the harder they worked. "Nobody cares what you know, until they know that you care." My boss at Cargill at the time, John Geisler, referenced to me this quote from Teddy Roosevelt to remind me of the importance of understanding your employees and genuinely caring about them. When you do, employees will follow you and consistently give you their best work.

CHAPTER 3
Research and the
Goodness Pays Score (GPS)

"Without data, you are just another person with an opinion."

Jeff Dufresne, former Marketing Director at
Procter & Gamble

As a successful business leader with Procter & Gamble (P&G) and Cargill, Paul Hillen learned the importance of validating his hypotheses, ideas, and hunches with research. It's what his seasoned business colleagues regularly expected. No data; no credibility.

So, before we started this book, Hillen warned: "I don't believe in 'soft benefits' or 'soft subjects.' I believe meaningful efforts and practices can and should be quantified and supported with facts. If you can't prove it and measure it, then can you really advocate for it?" Hillen's prove-it-to-me orientation came from the teaching of Jeff Dufresne, his most influential boss at P&G. So naturally, when Hillen first heard the words "goodness pays" from me as his executive coach, he responded with skeptical caution. *"I'll need some data to really be convinced,"* he thought to himself.

It was that phrase, *"Without data, you are just another person with an opinion,"* that grabbed my attention. Lots of people describe themselves as a "coach." But to get the highest credibility in the coaching business, a coach's opinion and experience needs to be supported by data. That's why Hillen was a perfect partner for this work because he's a seasoned skeptic. I'm an eternal optimist who takes most everything at face value. We make each other better leaders, thinkers, and writers.

Fast forward to today. For this book, we applied the "prove it" dynamic to our idea that "goodness pays," and here's the most basic finding:

> Goodness in business leadership positively
> impacts financial performance.

That sounds fantastic, right? Who wouldn't be in favor of getting consistently positive financial performance? And to think that it's linked with goodness? If you are curious, following is how we identified the correlation between goodness and financial performance.

Our Research Hypothesis

To test our hypothesis that goodness pays, we selected a high-quality research partner in SMS Research Advisors, a global market research firm nearing its 30th year in business. SMS, which has conducted several types of research projects for a wide variety of Fortune 500 firms, specializes in providing "Voice of the Customer (VOC)" insights, a partner business model that combines SMS's research expertise with the client's business segment expertise. The research portion of this book was based on a combination of the authors' business leadership experience and the research expertise of SMS.

The research goal was to prove what I have seen in my personal business practices and those of other leaders I admire most: *Leaders who demonstrate goodness with their employees and customers produce better financial results for their companies.*

Three-Phased Research Approach

To prove or disprove our hypotheses, we created a three-phased approach to our research. *Phase one* was a secondary literature review analysis of important leadership books and articles to inform our research team about the qualities and characteristics of good leadership. This was necessary to confirm SMS would be asking the right research questions. The literature review also ensured we were not out to prove or write about a concept that had already been proven, disproven, or explained in another publication.

In this first phase we found that no one else has specifically written about the concept of goodness in relationship with financial performance in any academic or popular business leadership literature. While there are some business/leadership books that allude to goodness-related behaviors, none empirically tie the specific goodness behaviors of their leaders to better financial results. This phase also helped us identify highly credible, contemporary leaders who we approached for interviews.

Phase two involved qualitative interviews with 15 executive leaders identified for their exemplary business results *and* leadership goodness. The former was easily determined by reviewing the recent financial performance of our prospective interviewees' companies. The latter, leadership goodness, was based on personal input from the employees of these leaders, input from their industry peers and competitors, and input from third-party endorsements and recognition by the news media and business associations (e.g. executive-of-the-year type awards).

We interviewed a representative group of leaders by industry, company size, geography, and gender:

Large company leaders (500+ employees):

- Amanda Brinkman, Chief Brand and Communications Officer at Deluxe

- Richard Davis, retired CEO and Chair at U.S. Bank

- Ray Kowalik, CEO at Burns & McDonnell

- Greg Page, retired CEO and Chair at Cargill

- Chris Policinski, retired CEO at Land O' Lakes

Mid-sized company leaders (250-499 employees):

- Lynn Casey, Chair at Padilla

- Jerry Mattys, CEO at Tactile Medical

- Mike McMahan, President at St. Francis Hospital

- Marcia Page, Founding Partner and Executive Chair at Värde

- Liz Smith, President at Assurance Agency

Small company leaders (50-249 employees):

- Charles Antis, CEO at Antis Roofing & Waterproofing

- Karen Clark Cole, CEO at Blink UX

- Umit Nasifoglu, President at Wedding Day Diamonds

- Clara Shih, CEO at Hearsay Systems

- Colleen Needles Steward, CEO at Tremendous! Entertainment

With thoughtful reflection on both their successes and failures, the leaders we interviewed shared vivid comments about how goodness pays in their leadership. Here's a sampling:

> *"If you really do treat your employees with value and respect, they're going to be more productive and your business is ultimately more profitable,"* said Karen Clark Cole, CEO at Blink UX, an acclaimed, Seattle-based digital research and design firm. Started nearly 20 years ago, Blink has grown tremendously in recent years, experiencing a minimum of 25 percent year-over-year revenue growth. Yet the company has still retained its original employee-centric culture.

> *"I never want to be the kind of leader who is out of touch with the work and her employees,"* said Clark Cole, honored in 2016 as an "Enterprising Woman of the Year" by Enterprising Women magazine. *"For me, it's about creating the right environment so that our people can thrive, they're getting feedback and they're clear on their roles and responsibilities. If our employees feel like they're positively contributing to the world, then they go home at the end of the day feeling valued, and they're in turn a better husband, wife, parent, and neighbor."*

Quantitative Research Highlights

Phase three was the quantitative research; a 900-person statistically significant survey of representative business leaders from across the United States, randomly chosen, and each asked the same set of 23 questions by SMS researchers. Of our 900-person sample, 300 came from large companies (500+ employees), 300 from medium companies (250-499 employees), and 300 from small companies (50-249 employees). We were able to examine survey results based on the company size of our respondents.

By asking open-ended questions that allowed survey participants to provide their own insights, we gathered data on the behaviors which exemplified goodness, what goodness looked like in successful leaders, and determined whether these behaviors impacted the financial results of the organization. We examined how goodness led to the highest identified level of success: *thriving*. Meaning, when an individual or organization is meeting all of their goals they are thriving. We set the bar high to understand what it takes for both leaders and their organizations to thrive. Sample questions included:

- If a leader you respect told you "goodness pays," what types of behaviors and outcomes would you expect to see from them?

- If you heard someone say "good leaders thrive," what behaviors and outcomes would you expect a good leader to demonstrate in order to thrive?"

- If someone was to say their organization's leader "radiates goodness," what types of behaviors and outcomes would you expect to see?

A more detailed description of our research findings are available in a white paper by contacting info@goodleadership.com

The summary of our analysis confirmed when good leaders have these five factors alive in their leadership, they consistently meet their financial goals. We call them the **Five Goodness Pays Factors:**

1. Compelling business plan.

2. Belief that profits are healthy for all.

3. Team-based culture.

4. Timely and transparent decision-making.

5. Magnetic ethics.

The key for making goodness pay in any organization is ensuring the Five Goodness Pays Factors are present on a consistent basis–not a once-in-a-while thing. You will read significantly more about these five factors in the following chapters.

One-Question Goodness Pays Score (GPS)

Perhaps the most exciting conclusion from the research is how one simple question can be a reliable predictor of how likely goodness will pay in your organization. The research analysis yielded a highly powerful one-question tool any leader can use to assess predictability in achieving positive financial results. Here is the question:

> Using a 1-10 scale: How would you rate your direct leader on proactively promoting goodness in his/ her decision-making within your organization?

Not only does GPS stand for the Goodness Pays Score, but most people today have come to know this acronym more commonly for Global Positioning System–a tool to help get you to your destination, by driving or walking. We believe this is a fitting analogy for the Goodness Pays Score because the GPS can show a new pathway for leaders to arrive at their business destinations.

I'm particularly excited about the GPS, because today's business leaders have learned to depend on simple surveys to provide valuable information for their business dashboards. These simple survey tools have become popular, if for no other reason than they are short:

- The 12-question Gallup Q12 Employee Engagement Survey

- The one-question Customer Effort Score (CES), from Surveypal–"How easy it is to do business with our company?"

- The one-question Net Promoter Score (NPS), developed by Bain & Company–"How likely is it that you would recommend our company/product/service to a friend or colleague?"

The GPS has similar potential to the NPS as a vital business tool because it is completely free, can be used without limitations, and it is simple to apply in any business. Today, more than two-thirds of Fortune 1000 companies use the one-question Net Promoter Score survey. "As a marketer, I love the simplicity of the NPS," shared Paul Hillen. "However, once I got my NPS score from the survey, we were never sure what we needed to do to improve our score. A low NPS number left us equally motivated to improve and also confused."

The objective in creating the GPS was to develop an easy tool to assess your leadership goodness, but more importantly, to also provide specific suggestions to improve financial success. Here is the fundamental basis for the GPS:

Higher Goodness Pays score = higher probability of consistently positive financial results

How Does the GPS Work?

The GPS is based on a single response from the direct reports of senior leaders within a company, business unit, department, function, or work group. For GPS statistical accuracy, we suggest the initial survey group should consist of at least 50% of your qualified respondents participating in this one-question survey. Of course, 100% is desired and recommended (especially with smaller organizations of 10 individuals or less), but a minimum of 50% participation should give you an accurate account. Additionally, like most surveys, to get honest feedback, we suggest using a survey tool that protects the anonymity of the respondents.

The GPS is calculated based on your employee responses to this *one key question*:

Using a 1-10 scale: How would you rate your direct leader on proactively promoting goodness in his/her decision-making within your organization?

We found that organizations whose leaders' average *GPS score was 9-10* are more likely to have increased revenues under the current leadershsip. In fact, 81% of leaders who scored 9-10 on this question reported an increase in year on year revenue in their organizations, while 18% saw revenue stay the same versus the previous year.

Organizations with an average score between 9 and 10 <u>on this one question</u> are more likely to be led by individuals we call **Goodness Accelerators,** leaders exhibiting others-focused behaviors such as teamwork, empathy, and sincerity. The research indicates this question is a predictor of good leadership and is a driver for increasing or maintaining financial expectations.

Conversely, organizations whose leaders' average *GPS score was 1-6* are significantly more likely to have decreasing–or at best unpredictable–financial performance. These companies are typically populated by individuals we call **Goodness Drainers,** leaders who exhibit self-focused, toxic behaviors such as self-promotion, closed-mindedness, and possible leadership incompetency. Good leaders consider both financial and non-financial indicators.

Additionally, employees working with **Goodness Drainers** place a higher emphasis on honesty, ethics, and fairness as leadership criteria. They think leaders should focus on the team and others versus making it about themselves. Further, employee responses under these drainers suggest their leader is not meeting the baseline criteria for goodness, defined as behaving ethically.

Organizations with a *GPS in the 7-8 range* are neutral and neither active **Goodness Accelerators** (as with 9-10 scorers) or **Goodness Drainers** (like the 1-6 scorers). This "neutral" group likely has untapped potential, which can be optimized for better financial performance by learning more about good leadership and how goodness improves financial results.

As noted previously, we conducted the survey with small, mid-sized, and large companies. The research showed that input from companies of all three sizes correlated the goodness behaviors of their leaders with increased financial results. The data shows that greater than 50% of companies that reported increased business performance had a GPS of 9-10, and more than 90% scored 7 or above. This clearly indicates that companies and leaders who demonstrate goodness behaviors get better financial results. All from one question.

Caution for Mid-Sized Businesses

While companies from all three size groups scored over 50%, as noted above in our GPS test, there is a bit of empirical caution. As explained previously in this chapter, our 900-person quantitative survey was split evenly among three sizes of businesses: 300 came from large companies (500+ employees), 300 from mid-sized companies (250-499 employees), and 300 from small companies (50-249 employees). In our survey results, we noted that mid-sized businesses are statistically significantly less likely (53%) to benefit financially from engaging in goodness-oriented leadership practices than with small (62%) and large (63%) businesses. (See chart below.) Medium-sized businesses which are goodness-oriented can still achieve positive financial results, but it is statistically less likely to happen than with small and large businesses.

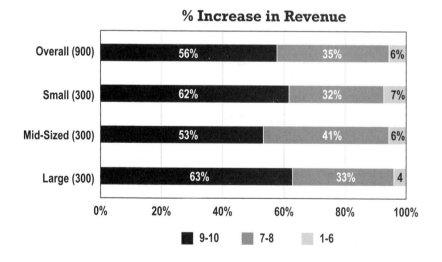

% Increase in Revenue

	9-10	7-8	1-6
Overall (900)	56%	35%	6%
Small (300)	62%	32%	7%
Mid-Sized (300)	53%	41%	6%
Large (300)	63%	33%	4

Why the disparity with mid-sized businesses? Two size-related reasons explain why: First, mid-sized businesses are often under tremendous internal and external operational scrutiny for everything from revenue growth to head count, making it more challenging–but not impossible–for leaders within such companies to practice goodness-centric leadership. We have found the scrutiny and pressure is usually driven by the fact that mid-sized companies have a greater need for cash as they try to grow fast. Second, mid-sized companies that have grown from a small company are often no longer able to rely on the positive charisma of a company founder or CEO–as is frequently the case with a small company–and do not typically have the internal employee development and engagement resources of a larger company.

So, if you are a leader within a mid-sized company, know that, as your business continues to grow and change, you will likely find adopting and adhering to goodness-oriented principles may be one of your greatest leadership challenges. But don't be discouraged. From our experience we believe exhibiting goodness behaviors can be the accelerator for taking your mid-sized company to the next level of financial success.

The GPS–An Example

Let's take a look at how the one-question GPS is calculated. If you are a leader and have 56 people in your organization, the 56 employees become the respondents. Through a simple anonymous written or online survey (e.g. Qualtrix or SurveyMonkey), ask each of the employees to answer the single question. To make the survey reliable, we highly recommend you get at least 50% to respond. To get the most participation and honest responses, I suggest you spend time to communicate the importance of their involvement and remind them the survey is anonymous.

In the example below, 51 out of 56 employees responded for a 91% response rate.

Calculating Goodness Pays Score (GPS)

Score employees gave their leader on the one question	Number of responses in the organization for each score	Leader scores multiplied by number of responses for each score	Percent of responses for each score	Average (total of scores divided by number of responses) 321 ÷ 51
1	0	0	–	
2	0	0	–	
3	0	0	–	This organizations Goodness Pays Score (GPS) =
4	3	12	6%	
5	8	40	16%	**6.29**
6	19	114	37%	
7	13	91	25%	
8	8	64	16%	
9	0	0	–	
10	0	0	–	
TOTAL	**51**	**321**		

This organization's Goodness Pays Score (GPS) is 6.29, putting it at the top of the 1-6 range. We'll explain below the significance of the scoring ranges and what we recommend as next steps for organizations in each of the ranges.

Supplementing Your GPS

Once you implement the GPS tool, you'll likely ask yourself, "What does this mean?" and "Why did people answer the GPS question way they did?" Sometimes, this simple average method for calculating the GPS doesn't tell the real story. In the table above, we learn that most of the scores are in the middle of the range, which likely means the employees are seeing and feeling the organization's leadership through the same lens. And, with most of the scores at 6 or 7, we can see how improving just few leadership behaviors related to the Five Goodness Pays Factors will improve the GPS.

If you want to explore root causes of the results with deeper analysis, there are ten additional questions for a follow up survey to help you determine areas for improvement.

First, what does your GPS score mean?

GPS = 9-10 Your company is led by managers who are *Goodness Accelerators*

Check alignment–is the score in line with your level of happiness with your financial performance? If so, review the Five Goodness Pays Factors, and reinforce those behaviors so you maintain your momentum. Make the time to celebrate the goodness that is alive in your leadership by recognizing your organization for the successes you've accomplished together.

GPS = 7-8 Your company is led by managers who are *Goodness Neutral*

You have untapped potential. Assess your managers on the Five Goodness Pays Factors, and determine which areas are common to most that are strengths and improvement areas. Encourage all supervisors, managers, and executives to read the next five chapters of this book, searching for one or two good ideas to build more momentum for goodness.

GPS = 1-6 Your company is led by managers who are *Goodness Drainers*

A sufficient level of goodness is missing in your organization. Consider supplementing your initial GPS by administering a second survey (see below) to dig another layer deeper.

Second, why did people answer the GPS question the way they did?

Collecting responses to the following ten-question survey will help you focus your development energy on the highest-leverage areas:

Using a 1-10 scale: How would you rate the following 10 leadership factors in our organization?

DISAGREE ▼ | 1 | 2 | 3 | 4 | 5 | 6 | 7 | 8 | 9 | 10 | AGREE ▼

1 I find our business plan to be compelling.

2 My fellow employees are genuinely excited about our business.

3 Our culture has a healthy respect for profits.

4 Employees believe they financially share in our company's profitability.

5 Team accomplishments are rewarded greater than individual accomplishments.

6 Redundant follow-through systems are present to ensure the most important work gets done.

7 Leaders are transparent with decision-making, consistently explaining the "why?" behind decisions.

8 Employees get the information they need, when they need it, to do their best work.

9 We have an ethical culture that attracts good people to our business.

10 Leaders live up to the same standards they expect of others.

As with the simple one-question GPS, the responses can be averaged to identify the level of agreement with these important factors aligned with goodness. The following chapters in this book provide insight and coaching tips to help improve agreement on all ten questions.

The main point: if you want to be a good leader who radiates goodness, but your GPS is not a 9-10, then we suggest you step back and re-examine your motives:

1. Do you want to be a good leader to help **you** be successful or to help **your company and employees** be successful?

2. Do you want to be a good leader only because it makes you feel good, or is it about being a good leader to help the team?

3. Are you emotionally invested in the company's future, or your own future?

Good leaders are allowed to want to personally benefit from their leadership and goodness, but what seems to differentiate a "5" score from a "10" score is if these leaders are also focused on bringing others up with them. Leaders who are invested in creating "goodness" only for themselves or purely for profit tend to lose revenue–and potentially respect. The research is clear on this point.

The Skeptic's Shift

Paul Hillen

I was never originally a big fan of the one-question Net Promoter Score (NPS). As mentioned in this chapter, I struggled with it because we only got a score, with no idea of what actions to take to improve our score. I'm a believer that you should not do market research unless you can identify what business decisions you will make as a result of the research. I struggled with what to do with a result that told me, *"Only 42% of your current customers would recommend your business."* Ok, so what do I do with that? How do I act on that data?

Well, I eventually made the shift, because, like most good research, you have to go deeper than just one question. To really understand what is behind the one question of whether your customers would recommend your business to others, you have to ask: *"Why did they answer it that way?"* Every time I used the NPS, I always used several questions that followed that one question. When I did, I uncovered the root cause.

Our one-question Goodness Pays Score (GPS) is no different. We strongly recommend that you ask more questions, either in the same survey, or as a follow-up survey. This will be important to understand why your employees rate you the way they do on your goodness leadership, how they define goodness, and what key behaviors they see that either detract or add to their perception of you as a good leader. You can start with the ten questions provided in this chapter.

So, if you are skeptical that just one question can possibly help you understand if goodness pays in your leadership style, you should be. The one-question GPS is just a start to understand where you are. Asking more questions to gain deeper insight, followed by coaching and changes in your leadership style, will be critical to increasing your business results.

The value of determining your organization's GPS will either support and reinforce the inherent goodness in your leadership practices (9-10) or it will be a catalyst to introduce and improve upon your goodness practices (8 or less). In Chapters 4-8, you will read about immediately applicable ways to demonstrate goodness in your leadership, which in turn will increase the likelihood of achieving your financial goals.

CHAPTER 3.5
Putting it All Together

"I don't know if you can be more good, but you can understand how your behaviors can create more good outcomes."

Richard Davis, retired CEO and Chair at U.S. Bank

What's up with half-a-chapter, as in "3.5"? It's not enough informa-tion for a bona fide chapter, but it is important information. If you care about how the coaching recommendations were created for the next five chapters, this half-chapter is for you. Otherwise, you can skip ahead.

The Goodness Pays Score (GPS) comes with a set of Five Goodness Pays Factors to consider as recommendations for how to improve your GPS:

 Compelling business plan.

 Belief that profits are healthy for all.

 Team-based culture.

 Timely and transparent decision-making.

 Magnetic ethics.

In chapter 3, we linked how the more these five factors are present in your organization, the more likely that goodness will pay financially for you.

The Five Goodness Pays Factors were identified by cross-referencing these <u>four</u> sources of extensive research:

- The literature review, phase 1

- The 15 high-quality leader interviews, phase 2

- The 900-person quantitative online survey, phase 3

- Input from more than 250 senior executive coaching engagements over an eight-year period at Good Leadership Enterprises

The fourth source is significant. The mix of coaching includes 34% CEOs and business owners, 40% senior executives, and 26% managers and emerging leaders. All were attracted to the Goodness Pays point of view because the coaching is designed to help good leaders improve each day. In aggregate these are high-performing leaders with teams who are willing to sharpen their aspirations, improve their ability for intellectually honest self-assessment, and to deepen their understanding of how leading with goodness can help them grow into the person they want to be, personally and professionally.

The next five chapters in *How Goodness Pays* focus on each of the Five Goodness Pays Factors and will help you answer the question: *"How do I make goodness pay for my organization?"* Each of these five chapters end with a ***Coaching Corner*** of immediately actionable steps and solutions you can implement to build goodness within your organization.

CHAPTER 4
Goodness Pays Factor 1: Compelling Business Plan

"Success today is about involving your people in creating a vision that is compelling. When that happens, employees are telling the story in their own voice and talking about our business in ways that are exciting to them, not just exciting for me as their leader."

Karen Clark Cole, CEO at Blink UX

It's been said that if we do not choose to plan, we leave it to others to plan for us. However, another problem in business planning is when we choose to do too much of the planning ourselves and fail to sufficiently include the key input of others. It's a mistake because it compromises the plan's motivational effectiveness.

Businesses with clear, compelling business plans built through the input of important implementers are more aligned with goodness and more likely to achieve profit goals. It stands to reason, as employees who contribute to building the plan are more likely to understand where they fit, and why they matter in the business. And that clarity creates excitement and motivation for employees to give their best effort for achieving the most important goals.

Still, there are business leaders who think business planning is a waste of time–valuable time that might be better spent building the business. But, multiple studies have shown the cause and effect correlation between business planning and profitability. Companies that plan grow 30% faster and are more successful than those that do not, according to a report in the *Journal of Management Studies*. Similarly, a study of more than 11,000 businesses, published in the *Journal of Business Venturing*, showed planning improved business performance. These studies also showed how collaborative business planning benefitted existing businesses even more than startups.

No matter your business, our research shows that a critical step toward achieving better business results is to build a compelling business plan which generates followership to deliver it. As the motivational expert Dale Carnegie once wrote: "There is only one way…to get anybody to do anything; and, that is by making the other person want to do it." The research for this book identified "communicates a clear vision with compelling strategies and goals" as one of the key behaviors of good leaders who get better financial results–it's the *"pays"* part of *Goodness Pays*.

Consider: If your leader tells you where the company is going, what the aspirational end-state looks like, and provides the resources and plan to get there, including your role in that plan, wouldn't you be busting through a wall to follow that leader? There's probably a good chance you would because your leader has shared with you where you fit in the plan and why you matter to the company's future. Who wouldn't want to be part of a team with that kind of support and potential for success?

That said, why do so many business plans falter or fail? Here are the most common mistakes leaders make when creating business plans:

- *Building a plan with input from only a few senior leaders, at the exclusion of the key employees who are critical to executing the plan.*

- *Creating a plan too complicated for people to digest or remember, which isn't clear to employees where they fit in and how it benefits customers.*

- *Failing to properly assess their organization's ability to accomplish the plan they've just created.*

To address these common mistakes, here are corresponding strategies for creating a compelling business plan that generates genuine employee followership:

- *Involve a broad spectrum of people in the creation of the plan who are responsible for its execution.*

- *Create a plan which is simple, equally aspirational and realistic, and aligned with customers' needs.*

- *Clearly articulate the capabilities and specific people needed to execute the plan and deliver its goals.*

Let's look closer at these three elements that are needed to create a compelling business plan.

Build with the Right People

Involve a broad spectrum of people in the creation of the plan who are responsible for its execution.

To this day, I remember the words of Paul Hillen as he told me about an interaction with a colleague as their senior leadership team was presenting the company's new "Playing to Win" business plan. "On what planet will this work?" said the colleague, as he leaned over and whispered into Hillen's ear. Hillen later explained "Not only were we having a hard time following the direction of this plan, but the words rang hollow because they were not specific, and there did not seem to be cohesive themes that were connected. Most importantly, there was only a small, seemingly disingenuous mention of the customer, so superficial that no one really believed the leaders who crafted the plan understood or cared about the customer. The plan was flawed by being internally focused."

A similar scenario occurred when a client was asked to help develop a joint venture to bring two businesses together to create a third company. The idea for the joint venture was developed in a private setting by the two CEOs from the companies, because they believed the discussions needed to be confidential. But without input from the key business leaders of each company, the CEOs struggled to get the necessary buy-in for the plan to work. Soon after revealing their plans, the managers in both companies discovered the joint venture idea was unsustainable. Eventually, momentum died and it was scrapped, but not before consuming a significant amount of staff time and resources. The most tangible cost was an abrupt loss of trust and confidence within the key managers who were excluded from the planning in the first place.

If you've worked in business long enough, you've likely seen business planning events like these in which executives build their plans in a vacuum without gaining enough input from significant team members, especially those who report to the leadership team. More often than not, the mistake begins when a small group of top executives travel to a remote retreat center, hunker down and create a plan without getting the proper input of key employees. Then they announce their plans with great fanfare, to a lukewarm response. Why does this happen?

Recently, I was facilitating a leadership session with a group of middle managers at a large U.S. company. During a break, I heard two of them looking at their smartphones and laughing at pictures on their company's Instagram account. The photos showed the company's top senior leadership team together, drinking wine at a posh resort. "Why is that so funny?" I asked. "This happens every year, the things they dream up seldom make sense. But this year, we're all under a travel ban...I guess that doesn't apply to the top brass." The hypocrisy, and lack of broader involvement, was not lost on those middle managers.

"What gets in the way of creating exciting plans is what I call 'ivory tower syndrome,'" said Jeff Prouty, Chair and Founder at The Prouty Project, a management consulting firm that guides CEOs, executives, and next-generation leaders toward extraordinary results. "It seldom works for a small team of leaders to assume they can write the plan themselves because they know more than everyone else."

As we heard from Karen Clark Cole in her opening quote to this chapter, she believes the shortest route for making a business plan compelling is to involve enough of the right people in building it. The plan comes alive when those from multiple levels and multiple business disciplines are included in both the building and pressure-testing of the plan.

> Depending on the type and size of your business, you benefit from involving as many people in the development of your plan as possible. "We recommend getting everyone involved in the planning, from the 60-something-year-old receptionist to the 20-something-year-old college intern," Prouty continued. "The key is to get a cross-section of people involved, and from more sources: current customers, lost customers, employees, former employees, key stakeholders in the community, and even shareholders. Everyone has a perspective on your business, if asked the right questions, and their input can be valuable."

Dale Carnegie addressed this timeless opportunity for business planning inclusivity when he wrote more than 80 years ago: "People support a world they help create." Carnegie's wisdom has been carried forward by leaders who now approach planning by encouraging employees to expect answers to these important questions:

1. What's our purpose?

2. What are we trying to accomplish together?

3. Where do I fit?

4. How does my work matter?

These questions align perfectly with what most people call "employee engagement." It's a universal desire in the work world to want to know how your work matters–even at a company's highest levels. Who doesn't want to feel like they are an important part of the company's success? If employees don't see or feel how they are integral to the plan, they lose engagement, and either shut down on the job or start looking for another place to work.

In most organizations, there are generally a select group of individuals who are critical to the daily execution of driving business results. In large companies, those tend to be department or functional leaders (in finance, research and development, marketing, sales, operations, and human resources) who report to a senior leader in the C-suite. In mid-sized companies, these people are generally functional leaders who report directly to the CEO and are on the company's leadership team. Many are "player-coaches" who both help lead the organization and are involved in day-to-day operations. With smaller companies, these people are the critical few who the company's owner/founder/CEO relies on daily to realize the vision and play both a strategic and tactical role. In small companies, it makes sense to involve everyone in the planning.

If you've had a tight circle of people working on your plan in the past, why not consider opening your process and involving more people? Start right now. Grab a pen and list those in your organization whom you believe are necessary for your business planning and execution. Add in other high-performing individuals who are your subject matter experts and go-to resources when things really need to get completed. The latter might be a few levels removed from senior leadership, but that doesn't matter. You know you need them for your business to succeed, and maybe more importantly, you know their engagement is critical to your company being successful. It's also a good idea to involve your human resources lead and ask them who is on the company's "high potential talent list" so you involve the talent you want to retain and grow for the future.

Make it Simple, Concise, Realistic, and Customer Focused

Create a plan which is simple, equally aspirational and realistic, and aligned with customers' needs.

Many business plans are several pages long, filled with platitudes and clichés, are high-level, and don't show the integration needed between strategic planks and internal organizations to implement it. Often when I'm coaching senior executives, I ask to see their business plans so I can understand their challenges and where they want to take the company. More often than not, I see dull, 20-page black ink on white paper documents, or 50-slide PowerPoint decks. Yikes! When I'm handed one of those large plastic binders that says "Strategic Business Plan," I know how to help that company quickly improve its performance. The first step is to simplify.

Instead of using too many or meaningless words in your business plan, seek to make your plan come alive by being as clear, concise, and specific to your company as possible. Think it's not possible? Consider how a new business plan–just 270 words long–about the length of a single page of typed text–helped save a major American airline from certain failure.

In his classic *Harvard Business Review* article, "Right Away and All at Once–How We Saved Continental," former Continental Airlines President and COO, Greg Brenneman, shares how Continental CEO Gordon Bethune and he, with several key others in the company, ultimately saved 40,000 jobs at Continental by creating and executing a short, yet powerful, 270-word business plan called the "Go Forward Plan."

At the time, Continental was grappling with its third bankruptcy filing. The airline's eventual merger with United Airlines was 16 years away–and would never have happened if Brenneman and others hadn't crafted Continental's "Go Forward Plan." It featured four key components:

1. **Fly to Win**—designating which markets the company would serve.

2. **Fund the Future**—the company's financial plan to get there.

3. **Make Reliability a Reality**—the company's customer service plan to win with customers.

4. **Working Together**—the behaviors required of the company's employees to win.

As Brenneman noted, unlike previous Continental business plans which had failed, this plan needed to be simple and specific to the airline's situation. That meant no clichés or platitudes that could be applied to any other competitor, no wasted words, and, as with most newspapers and newscasts, written at an eighth-grade level for clarity. As he noted about the company's prior business plans: "You probably (previously) couldn't find a single employee, even among senior management, who could tell you the company's strategy."

Brenneman's observation is consistent with my experiences as an executive coach. As a standard practice prior to our firm facilitating leadership retreats, we interview the client company's senior managers. We consistently observe that senior managers, just one level below the senior executives, typically cannot recite the top three strategies or priorities of their companies–even when aided. As a result, we have learned by failing to communicate simply, many executive teams inadvertently create blind spots in their organizations which eat away at employee engagement and productivity, resulting in poorer financial results.

Continental found success with its new plan by keeping it artfully simple; the "Go Forward Plan" wasn't complex. "It was pure common sense," Brenneman said. "We needed to stop flying 120-seat planes with only 30 passengers on them. We needed to get people to their destinations on time with their bags. We needed to start serving food when people were hungry. We needed to create an atmosphere where people liked coming to work."

Despite a wealth of information now available to anyone in business, the best business plans are still elegantly simple, and created face-to-face among colleagues who know and respect each other. Keep in mind the essence of "excellence," no matter your line of business, is "simple, done well." The plan needs to communicate in easy-to-understand ways which generate agreement and buy-in among all employees in the business, in ways that everyone–even friends and family members of employees–can understand and be excited about.

To help you achieve the simplicity and clarity of business planning you need for your company, consider using a business planning tool which Paul Hillen began using at P&G, later taught at Cargill, and still uses today. It's called the Cascading Strategy approach, adopted from the Monitor Group. This tool shows how each key strategic element is independent so that it can be pressure-tested and executed on its own. It also ensures that the plan's strategies are interdependent to ensure that key connections are not missed. And by involving the right set of employees in the planning, these employees can communicate to others in their work groups why their work is critical to the success of the whole. As shown in the accompanying graphic, there are eight components to the cascading strategy tool Hillen uses:

1. **Vision**—The company's desired high-level end-state.

2. **Objectives**—Key metrics that can be measured to accomplish the vision.

3. **Goals**—Specific, measurable, and quantifiable financial and market based milestones, by year, at least three years into the future.

4. **Where to Play**—Specific choices of geography, customer channels, customer segments, products, services, technologies, and any other areas important to your business.

5. **How to Win**—How the company will specifically succeed (with its customers, and over the competition) for each of the "Where to play" choices. It's important that these strategies are unique to your company or they wont' be a lever to win.

6. **Action Plans**—Specific actions including who will do what to deliver each of the "Where to play" and "How to win" choices.

7. **Capabilities**—The amount and type of capabilities and number of people critical to each of the "Where to play" and "How to win" elements.

8. **Systems and Tools**—The systems and resources needed to achieve success. This should span all

functions–technology, operations, customer relationship management, etc.

The Model

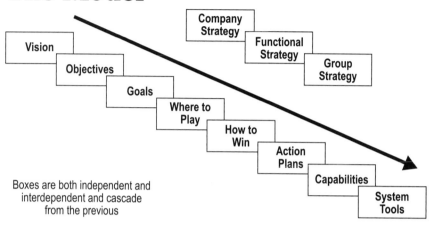

Boxes are both independent and interdependent and cascade from the previous

As a coach, what I like best about this model is the positive energy that's built into the words "play" and "win" that are central to the model. The best business leaders understand the key to winning is understanding where they are <u>not</u> going to compete. In addition to determining the choices of what you will do, the Cascading Strategy exercise identifies those choices of what the organization will not do, so that managers don't get distracted by surprise opportunities that are outside of the organization's strategic focus.

Besides ensuring your business plan matches the execution ability of your employees, you also need to be certain the plan aligns with the business interests and needs of your customers. This is a critical component of the "Where to play" and "How to win" sections of the Cascading Strategy. Both sections should include the customers you've chosen to serve and specifically how you will win with each segment. This is why customer research, input, and feedback is a must-do and a critical foundation to any compelling plan. That's precisely what Amanda Brinkman did, as chief brand and communications officer of Deluxe, a century-old company long known as the nation's dominant provider of paper checks, which today also provides marketing services to millions of small businesses.

Brinkman and her colleagues confronted a market reality: for at least two decades, futurists were predicting online banking and credit cards would eventually mean the end of paper check-writing. This hasn't happened yet, largely because many businesses still prefer to write checks to one another. Nonetheless, the paper check industry is slowly "declining"–something that Deluxe has long anticipated and has, for years, been deliberately evolving its offerings to address. In particular, the company made strategic investments in products and services to help small businesses with marketing, ranging from website development and hosting to logo design to email marketing. By many accounts, the evolution was successful: Deluxe became a growth engine for more than 4.4 million small businesses. But the company's brand awareness remained low.

So, on Deluxe's centennial, Brinkman and her colleagues knew they had to do something revolutionary. And to build a roadmap, they drew insights directly from the nation's small business owners.

"What we heard and saw, over and over again, was how passionate, proud and dedicated these small business owners were, as they faced increased competition from big-box retailers," Brinkman said. "These small business owners had the courage and grit to survive and thrive, and they were experts within their fields, but they desperately needed marketing help. Most entrepreneurs don't invest in their dreams because they don't want to do their marketing–so if we can help them with that piece, they can get back to doing what they love."

Small businesses comprise more than 30 million businesses and employ nearly half of all employees in the United States, according to the U.S. Small Business Administration, testifying as to why it made sense for Deluxe to continue to serve this business segment to meet its own business interests. And while Deluxe had evolved into a full-service marketing services and products partner, they needed to reach their target audience in an authentic way, if they wanted to transform their own brand.

On Deluxe's 100th anniversary, rather than focus on the company's past, they decided to shine a spotlight on their target market–small businesses–and the passionate people behind them. It was also an opportunity for Brinkman to put her "Do Well By Doing Good" philosophy to the test–a belief that all companies can make a meaningful impact in their consumers' lives, while also bolstering their bottom line.

Brinkman and her team made a bold bet on the "Small Business Revolution," a campaign that showcases the courage and determination of small business owners. The Small Business Revolution began by showcasing 100 small business stories across the country through photo essays, videos, and a documentary. Along the way, they saw that nowhere are small businesses more under siege than in small towns. So they launched "Small Business Revolution–Main Street"–which each year awards one small town and its small businesses a $500,000 revitalization, and chronicles the transformation in an acclaimed show that streams at SmallBusinessRevolution.org and on Hulu.

Suddenly, through the lens of the Small Business Revolution, Deluxe employees saw their connection to America's small businesses, beyond their legacy check business and into a future that is limitless. They also saw how they were part of a movement that was changing lives and entire communities. Embracing this marketing positioning was a critical business shift that made it possible for Deluxe to achieve ongoing positive revenue growth and profitability.

Can Your Organization Execute Your Plan?

Clearly articulate the capabilities and specific people needed to deliver the plan and its goals.

A big mistake leaders often make, perhaps out of raw optimism and cost realities, is to incorrectly assess the company's ability to deliver the articulated plan. It's easy to get inspired by the decisions associated with "Where to play" and "How to win," and forget to properly assess if your company has the current or even future ability to execute these plans. To address this need, our leadership coaches encourage clients in mid-sized and large companies to deploy what we call "Truth Teams." Small teams, made up of multi-level, multi-functional people are coached on how to test the feasibility of ideas and the degree of employee buy-in. Truth Teams are only possible in organizations which encourage their employees to be candid and truthful with their input, without fear of consequence or repercussion, no matter who created the idea.

Truth Teams engage colleagues in discussion about their level of agreement with these statements:

- I understand our vision and purpose.

- To achieve our vision, we have created a well-built plan with realistic goals.

- I am energized when I explain our plan and goals to others.

- Our plan is aligned to our customers' wants and needs.

The impact of a Truth Team exercise can be eye-opening. One CEO client commented "We've scaled back some of our new product development plans because of the Truth Teams, and dramatically accelerated others. But the biggest benefit since we've been using this internal testing strategy has been less implementation errors due to a much higher buy-in."

Think how often you've been part of a company whose business plan was launched without properly assessing the ability of the organization to execute on the plan's strategies. It shouldn't be a surprise that without completing this critical step, employees and managers in such companies get discouraged at some point during the business year, because the company is not achieving important goals, and the probability of meeting the year-end profit-sharing goal is diminishing.

Truth Team leaders need to have a reasonably detailed plan to share with colleagues before those colleagues can assess whether they agree or not. The key is for leaders involved in planning to adopt some form of activity system, which identifies and assesses the resources required for the plan's completion, and then helps map these resources to the plan's most important activities.

There are many planning systems available. The Entrepreneurial Operating System (EOS), developed by Gino Wickman, is described in his book *Traction*. The model is specifically designed to help small, entrepreneurial companies grow with better planning and accountability. The original Cascading Strategy model described by Paul Hillen is explained in the best-selling book *Playing to Win* by A.G. Lafley (former P&G CEO) and Roger L. Martin. Perhaps the most classic planning model is the McKinsey 7S, introduced in the 1980s by the management consulting firm McKinsey and Company. Plans such as these showcase why leaders can't make changes to an organization in isolation. Good leadership requires planning which shows how strategy, structure, skills, culture, staff, systems, and shared values are all interconnected.

> *Good leadership requires planning which shows how strategy, structure, skills, culture, staff, systems, and shared values are all interconnected.*

Whatever system you choose, assessing the plan plays a critical role in helping employees understand where they fit and how they matter, as we discussed earlier in this chapter. When the plan is simplified and refined on one page with employee input, leaders can show how each employee specifically plays a role, and how important each employee's daily activities are to the strategy.

More Business Planning Insights from Our Interviews

A key theme gained from the interviews for this book is how collaboration and engagement are core to how good leaders approach their business planning. The more people who are directly involved in the business plan, the more compelling this plan becomes to the employees. Here's what some of our other interviewees had to say on this subject:

- **Charles Antis, CEO at Antis Roofing & Waterproofing:** "I think traditional, top-down leadership and business planning is a model that can't survive. If you don't have excitement about a cause that rings with authenticity within your culture, then I don't think you will be relevant. How do you get that without involving your employees in setting the strategies and goals for the future?"

- **Jerry Mattys, CEO at Tactile Medical:** "The beauty of our business is that we touch patients every day. So, there's not a week that goes by that I don't get a call or an e-mail from a satisfied patient saying, 'You have changed my life with your equipment, with your service; your people are great!' To keep people engaged and involved, we play that back to the employees so they get a feel for how we're impacting lives positively. And we integrate that customer insight directly into our planning. I think a big part of our success is that I never let people forget that excitement."

- **Richard Davis, retired CEO and Chair at U.S. Bank**: "Over the course of my career, I discovered collaboration is the biggest thing to create excitement. I definitely am not one who wants to take credit for everything. I recognize we're a much greater company and a greater team when we get multiple perspectives and multiple opinions on how things should be done. When that happens, we have more excitement in the business, and our results are always better."

The Skeptic's Shift

Paul Hillen

I've always been a very organized, planful person. My senior year in college, I did a year-long internship with IBM, and then started my career at P&G after graduation. Both companies fit me like a glove–well-organized and process-oriented. That part did not require a shift in my thinking. What required a shift was involving a broader group of people.

My coaching at P&G involved large doses of strategic training. I was also surrounded by exceptional people. This led to a select few of us getting together, building the strategy and then deploying it broadly with others working on the brand. While we got good results, I now believe we could have been even more successful if we had involved functional leaders and key employees in developing those strategies.

Some reading this may think creating a compelling business plan is simply a waste of time. With tech start-ups popping up daily, and traditional business models being blown up at a similar pace, who has time to do a strategic plan? You might be thinking *"By the time I complete a plan, it will be obsolete because the pace of change is moving so fast."*

This is the mindset shift I'm asking you to make as a "contemporary skeptic." Take three days to begin building or revising your strategic plan.

If you are skeptical as to why, then answer these questions: "What is more important than spending time developing how you will win, how you will beat your competition, and what capabilities you need to do it? Is it not worth a comparatively small amount of your time within your fiscal year to ensure that you have a compelling plan to win in the marketplace, which excites your employees and leadership, and propels you toward working to thrive and accomplish it?"

If you decide not to take the time to prepare a plan, ask yourself one more question: "Am I letting the tyranny of the urgent take priority over the importance of the strategic?" Only you can answer that.

Coaching Corner

How Can You Get Better at Business Planning?

☑ **Involve high-potential young leaders in your planning**: Work with managers to develop criteria for identifying high potential talent to involve in your planning process. Consider assigning each person a senior level mentor to help them learn more about the business, and contribute unedited commentary as ingredients to the new plan. It might also be time to try a new planning format. The Cascading Strategy model described by Paul Hillen is a good way to get people involved. The tool's questions of "Where will we play?" and "How will we win?" are two good questions to engage emerging leaders in the strategic planning process. Have them give you their input on those two questions as a start.

☑ **Survey to find a baseline:** Anonymous online team surveys can help identify how people in your organization think and feel about your plan. For example, Good Leadership Enterprises offers what we call the "Team Momentum Survey" (available at goodleadership. com) to provide data about a team's enthusiasm and commitment (or lack thereof) for supporting a business plan. Team members indicate their agreement level with the four statements mentioned earlier this chapter in the discussion about Truth Teams:

- I understand our vision and purpose.

- To achieve our vision, we have created a well-built plan with realistic goals.

- I am energized when I explain our plan and goals to others.

- Our plan is aligned to our customers' wants and needs.

☑ **Build an internal "public scorecard" that can be viewed by all managers to track employee and company progress:** The principle behind an internal "public scorecard" is to allow more people in the business to be aware of and involved in achieving important goals. Sophisticated project management software is nice for communicating progress, but a simple spreadsheet or dashboard which employees can easily view and understand will work just as well. The key is reviewing progress on a monthly or quarterly cadence with managers and their teams, allowing people to build excitement, celebrate progress, assess where there is positive or negative momentum, and to agree on areas in the business plan where mid-course corrections are necessary. A simple traffic light labeling system can help evaluate progress toward important objectives: red=unacceptable progress, needs correction; yellow=almost meeting expectations, needs attention; and green=on track, needs celebration.

CHAPTER 5
Goodness Pays Factor 2:
Belief that Profits are Healthy for All

"Inconsistent profitability is a lack of good leadership, because people don't know the most important things to do, and they don't see pay-offs. Because of that, they don't feel motivated. It's really important that leaders help everyone see how working together will create a healthy win for everyone involved."

Clara Shih, CEO at Hearsay Systems

The Power of Talking About Profits

To properly discuss Goodness Pays Factor 2: Belief that profits are healthy for all, we cannot ignore the word "pays" in the term *Goodness Pays*.

To most people, the word "pays" means "money first" and other things second. Some leaders try to sidestep paying less money to their employees by providing other things instead, like free coffee and pizza parties, or Friday afternoons off during the summer. But for goodness to pay financially, it's most effective to provide those nice extras while also sharing profits with employees to create a company-wide focus on the bottom line. Employees can and will help ownership be profitable if they believe profitability is a two-way street that benefits all involved. The best employees think this way: "I will help you be profitable if I believe *we can both profit from the experience.*"

Colleen Needles Steward, CEO at Tremendous! Entertainment, summarized this idea during our interview: "The thing that has always impressed me about the leaders that I admire most is how generous they are. They are successful because they are generous with employees financially, and also with time, benefits, and resources. I've learned that it pays off huge. Employees are more loyal. They are more invested. They take the success of the company personally–it becomes their own mission–and that means you will be even more successful as a CEO."

> The best employees think this way: "I will help you be profitable if I believe we can both profit from the experience."

It is certainly working for Needles' company. In the last five years, revenue for Tremendous! Entertainment has more than quadrupled. Not surprisingly, Needles explained employee turnover at the company during this time period has been practically zero.

Compare and contrast the cultural experience at Tremendous! Entertainment with companies you know which are consistently ungenerous with their employees. Unfortunately, such organizations are not tough to find. In a 2016 global survey of 400,000 employees working in different sized organizations and industries, the consulting firm Aon learned that only 52% of men and 47% of women believe the results they get at work are connected to their pay. Small wonder, according to the survey, that a growing number of such employees, especially women, pose a flight risk. Who wants to work at a company that doesn't appear to treat its employees generously and fairly?

Healthy Profitability is About Sharing What Matters Most

As the examples above show, great results are possible when a company takes a healthy attitude about profitability and is open with its employees about its finances. A comment from our 900-person online survey highlighted how such a healthy attitude about profitability can help employees feel like winners. "It's a big deal to create a culture that both *respects* and *expects* profitability," said one of the survey-takers.

A focus group participant provided deeper insight on the same topic: "I've seen both sides of this equation. My first job was in the same industry as I am in today, but there was almost a disdain for profitability–mainly because the top executives did pep rallies when earnings and the stock price went up...but none of us saw extra pay, stock options, perks or anything. It felt unfair. I moved to this new firm because it was obvious that everyone on the team knew and cared about the profitability as a source of personal pride and benefit. This firm outperforms my prior firm in practically every meaningful measure."

What are those measures? Most people would consider the most *meaningful* measures to be consistent growth in revenue and profits, high employee and customer satisfaction, and consistently superior product/service quality. But for this discussion about goodness and good leadership, the driver that makes everything else *healthy* is consistently profitable growth. Think about the challenges or outright impossibility of creating any other positive workplace results if you haven't aligned your employees to your company's fundamental need for profitability, year after year, and how it benefits everyone.

Making the Connection: Healthy Profits are Healthy for All

Here is an easy equation for how good leaders can communicate the importance of profitability to employees:

Healthy company profits = more jobs
+ higher paying jobs
+ better benefits
+ bigger bonuses
+ higher contributions to pensions/ESOPs/401Ks
+ longer-term sustainability of the company

Looking at this equation, it is common sense that all of these positive results come about for employees if the company continues to grow its profits. However, as I've seen with all sizes of companies, this message often does not get through to employees. Instead, I hear from employees how they resent when executives celebrate better business results, because they feel as if only the senior leaders benefit from those results.

The problem lies in poor communication. The responsibility rests with leaders to communicate how healthy profits benefit everyone–from hourly employees to management.

Profits as the Special Sauce for a Sandwich Business

We can learn how the concept of leading with goodness really works from a small business restauranteur, Dan Balach, CEO at Lambi Corporation, whose firm runs 10 gourmet sandwich shops. The business today is fully dependent on its store managers to be successful, making it imperative that Balach and his leadership team consistently convey to these managers their value to the organization and its profitability. The managers in turn pass along this mindset to each shop's front-line employees.

"We give 30% of the net income to the management teams in the stores every four-week business cycle to keep everyone focused on profitability," Balach explains. It's a concept he learned early in his career, working in a totally different industry. "My first job was in sales in a very successful pharmaceutical company called Marion Labs. What I learned from the founder, Ewing Marion Kauffman, was the mantra: 'Those who produce, share in the profits.'" This philosophy is the *special sauce* for how Balach's stores outperform his peer group.

"When our managers first come to work for us, they don't understand why some months the profit-sharing bonuses are higher than others," he explained. But every month Balach reviews the P&L statement for each of his stores with the managers. It's a teaching role that he really enjoys.

"The moment when the managers accept accountability for their bonuses, they take significantly more pride in their work, and our companywide profitability becomes more consistent," he says. The main benefit to the business is spreading the responsibility for profits across a wider team of people, who, in turn, get to celebrate their successes with the other employees in their stores.

But the benefits to Balach's goodness-oriented approach extend beyond profitability to employee loyalty. That's critical in an industry that is traditionally viewed as low-loyalty/high-turnover.

Balach explains the importance of employee loyalty: "In an hourly wage business, it's easy for employees to think of the owner as the bad guy. We can't afford to have any fear in the stores, because people just quit and find a job around the corner with someone else." So, the culture of Balach's sandwich shops needs to be built around regularly sharing successes with employees when the store is successful on a daily, weekly, and monthly basis.

"Everyone knows that when the store bonuses are low, so is my bonus as the owner," Balach smiled. "So now when we come into the store with questions and coaching, they all know it's because we want everyone to thrive together."

The Four Drive Model

The concept of *"profits are healthy for all"* does not mean leaders *always* need to distribute more money to employees in the form of bonuses or pay raises when profitability is strong. Studies have shown for decades that employees also value other factors in their jobs to consider their jobs to be healthy.

Kurt Nelson, PhD, is President of The Lantern Group, a management consulting firm, which for 20 years, has been at the forefront of applying behavioral science to improving the effectiveness of people at work. From a psychological perspective, Nelson explains how profits can be healthy for everyone–even if they don't always translate into a direct additional monetary benefit for everyone.

"Psychologists long ago identified the concept of people needing both intrinsic and extrinsic benefits to satisfy their basic need to feel appreciated," Nelson said. "*Intrinsic* rewards, in the context of a healthy workplace, are about ensuring employees are doing work they love, feeling the satisfaction of a job well done, and knowing the organization is winning in the marketplace. *Extrinsic* includes the financial gains of bonuses, dividends, or profit-sharing contributions–as well as commemorative plaques celebrating specific goals."

Understanding the difference between intrinsic and extrinsic rewards can help you understand why hosting something like a lunchtime pizza party can also be an important part of a healthy workplace culture. However, over-relying on things like parties falls short if monetary rewards are not also included. Nelson explains this fact by citing the Four Drive Model, which was first introduced in 2008 by Harvard University Researchers Nitin Nohria, Boris Groysberg, and Linda-Eling Lee:

- Drive #1 is **Acquire & Achieve**—This includes our need for things, status, and resources, which includes money. "It's number one, because it's very important, and it explains why the 'feel good' type of rewards are not enough to create ongoing high performance and consistent profitability," Nelson said.

- Drive #2 is **Bond & Belong**—This is our need to create positive relationships, engage with people we enjoy, and to "fit in."

- Drive #3 is **Create & Challenge**—This is our need to create, improve, master, learn, and overcome challenges.

- Drive #4 is **Defend & Define**—This is our need to defend ideas and relationships, which are tied to our sense of a larger purpose.

Some leaders understand these four drives naturally, others benefit from learning and applying each of the drives in specific ways. "We've seen organizations increase profitability the most when leaders satisfy all four underlying drives, and intentionally strive to meet those needs," Nelson said. "Financial rewards for employees are important to consistent profitability, but financial rewards alone will not lead to the concept of employees perceiving profitability as healthy for everyone in the business," he said. "We also have to satisfy the other three drives."

Consistent with the validity and accuracy of the Four Drive Model, Needles Steward shared the following:

"I think the more ways we find to engage the motivations of our workforce, the more our managers and employees take the success of the company personally," she said. "The goal is for our mission to become their own mission. It doesn't happen overnight. We've seen that it takes about two years for people to learn where they fit in, to make friends here, feel invested and find their own internal rewards. But when they adopt a 'this is our company,' attitude, as opposed to Colleen's company or the shareholders' company, those rewards come alive in everything. Including our profitability."

To check how your leadership aligns with the four drives, you can use these four questions to see if profitability is seen as healthy for all:

1. Do employees have specific financial rewards beyond salary for doing things that lead to increased profitability?

2. Do employees feel like they fit into a team that they enjoy?

3. Are employees continuously learning from meaningful work experiences?

4. Do employees have a sense of personal identity in the organization's mission, so much so that they will defend their team and the purpose?

Even in Tough Times

At this point, you might think "Sure, it's easy to be generous with employees when times are good are things are going well. But what about when times are tough?" Actually, having a workplace culture of generosity can pay off the most when times seem the darkest.

"Just before the economy crashed in 2009, our firm had adopted a high growth strategy. And high growth requires a lot of cash," said Jerry Mattys, CEO at Tactile Medical. "Very soon into the recession, it became obvious to me that keeping up with our aggressive growth meant we were going to run out of money at a time when it would be terribly onerous to try to raise money again."

So, Mattys and his management team decided the best strategy to preserve the financial health of Tactile Medical would be for all of the employees, including leadership, to take a 20% pay cut to free up cash. Basically, Mattys was asking everyone to provide a bridge loan to the company by foregoing salary dollars in order to increase the company's chance of survivability.

Surprisingly to Mattys, it felt good to be candid with his employees about the company's financial needs and their role in helping shape the company's future. It helped that Mattys and his team had built a healthy workplace culture in which employees could communicate openly and honestly about their intentions.

"It may sound strange to hear, but I actually felt good as a leader communicating with everyone, 'All of us are going to take a 20% pay cut for the rest of the year, myself included,'" Mattys said. "It was important to be transparent, and to share in the financial condition of the company, knowing full well that if we didn't hit our milestones, we weren't getting that 20% back. It was a great learning experience, and a motivator because we were in it together." Goodness did pay for Mattys and Tactile Medical employees because the 20% was paid back at the end of the year when they achieved their goals.

We heard a similar story from a professional services firm president, who found a way to motivate his employees to pour their heart and soul into a turnaround. Following the 9/11 attacks, most of the firm's client contracts were suspended or canceled, imperiling the firm's finances.

In response, the firm's owners created a special incentive program encouraging an all-hands-on-deck effort to pull the firm out of its financial crisis. Similar to Tactile Medical, one strategy was a mandatory, company-wide furlough in which all employees agreed to work just four days a week for three months, without being paid for the fifth day. The firm's owners also agreed to work for no salary at all during this time to preserve the company's cash. The non-owner employees were willing to share in the "pain" of a voluntary, temporary 20% pay reduction because of the firm's history of generosity, and because they saw the owners forego their own pay for the benefit of all.

When it became clear the business would recover, the owners consulted a small group of employees to develop a plan to reward their resilience. A veteran employee chimed in: "One of my friends went on a cruise with her firm when they accomplished a huge stretch goal. I'm not interested in celebrating the fact that our business survived. It was our job to do the right thing and save the company. What I'd like to do is to take the whole company to a Caribbean resort when we hit a new stretch goal."

The next February, after beating their financial goal by 10%, the firm's owners and employees celebrated together on a warm Caribbean beach, knowing that their collaborative, mutually beneficial efforts had made it all possible.

Creating a Sense of Ownership

What the two previous stories describe is the importance of instilling a sense of ownership in employees so that they treat decisions about the company as if they were owners themselves. That's a significant and powerful mindset.

However, among companies owned by their employees, known as ESOP companies, a sense of personal ownership is business as usual. ESOP, which stands for Employee Stock Ownership Plan, literally puts a company's ownership in the hands of employees. ESOP companies first became popular in the 1970s as waves of first-generation business owners sought a tax-advantaged way to transfer ownership to a next generation of owners.

Since Congress established the ESOP tax structure for businesses in 1974, ESOPs have routinely outperformed businesses with other ownership structures. Why? It's not because of the tax advantages, but because of the sense of ownership it instills in employees.

"It's pretty well documented that ESOP companies generally outperform companies with other ownership structures," said Ray Kowalik, CEO at Burns & McDonnell, one of the fastest-growing engineering firms in the country, and an ESOP company.

"We think of ownership in the hands of the employees as our special sauce," Kowalik said. "All of our employees are developed with the idea they are making decisions every day that need to be right for the whole entire organization."

ESOPs have specific tax advantages when one generation of owners transfers ownership to the next generation. The disadvantage of ESOPs is that the government recognizes the ownership structure as a retirement plan that requires government regulation. It takes a unique management team to embrace the idea of the government regularly looking under the hood, so to speak, to inspect the engine of the business. And, with all of the federal regulatory protocols that must be followed, the expenses of maintaining an ESOP can be significant.

That said, the cultural benefits of being an ESOP firm–or acting like one, in terms of employee behaviors–can be invaluable, according to Kowalik. "I believe *the feeling of ownership* as a core principle is a building block that leaders should be able to leverage in any industry, whether the company is an ESOP or not," he said.

"Here's what I see, as I consult with other companies," Kowalik continued. "When there's a fire, a lot of people who don't feel ownership run away, and say it was somebody else's fault. They're not going to be found anywhere near the fire. But when employees feel ownership, everybody runs to the fire, and sees what they can do to help. They don't waste time blaming anybody. They just go try to fix it."

It's not the ESOP legal structure itself that creates an employee's feeling of ownership. It's more about leaders cooperating and helping each other, being transparent with financial information, and sharing profitability with their employees.

"We were an ESOP until August 2018. I don't think that gave us any particular advantage, since we shared financial information as well as profits long before we created the ESOP," said Lynn Casey of Padilla, one of the nation's largest independently owned public relations firms. "In the early days of the ESOP, we were a collection of individuals. We didn't automatically have the spirit of collective ownership. We were like we all had our own barber chairs that generated fees. But when we wanted to grow faster, we weren't thinking about growth in the same way. It was more like individual ownership."

"The growth came when we focused on creating that collective ownership, leading together, behaving more like a full service spa where all of our services combined could offer a lot more to our clients," Casey continued. "When that happened our collective pride grew, and so did our business. It's not the legal ESOP structure that creates the success. It's the feeling of collective ownership, the 'we're all in this together' spirit that makes the difference for us."

Mattys, who earlier shared his financial crisis story, also emphasized that an ESOP structure is not required to help employees feel like owners. "The way we lead around here helps attract to the table a group of people at the senior level who act like the owners of the company," he said. "We are transparent with our financials, and we include people in important discussions about the business. So, when the decisions need to be made, and I'm not around to make them, we're okay, because I know they're going to make decisions as if they own the company. It's a great feeling."

An Important Distinction

One of the biggest mistakes that damages an employee culture is when a company's owners and executives get payouts in the same year that layoffs, big cost-cuts, frozen merit increases, or no financial bonuses occur for employees. This most often happens in mid-sized companies with complex ownership structures in which management has a voracious need for cash to meet the return expectations of its owners. But that doesn't make it any less palatable to the employees who learn about such disparities.

While it's understandable for a company's owners to get paid, for goodness to truly "pay," leaders need to embrace the idea that collaboration means sharing. And to have consistent profitability, leaders need to consistently share their profits.

Nelson makes the point this way: "Employees will fight long and hard for a company they believe in and one that has their back. But the moment they sense deceit or feel betrayed, those same

To have consistent profitability, leaders need to consistently share their profits.

employees can turn into the biggest liability in the company. At the very least, the best talent will leave."

The theme of building commitment to the idea that profits are healthy for all is evident in the following quotes from our interviews.

More Healthy Profits Insights

- **Umit Nasifoglu, President at Wedding Day Diamonds:** "I think about money as the driving force. It's a good scorekeeper to keep me honest as a leader. So, good leadership has allowed us to have good people that pay attention to profitability to give us the comfort to do the right things in the business."

- **Liz Smith, President at Assurance Agency:** "Profitability is one of the key metrics in any organization. And you will be successful in this area if you're not worried about your own personal success or personal acknowledgement; instead focusing your efforts on your team winning and getting most excited when that happens."

- **Karen Clark Cole, CEO at Blink UX:** "(At) Blink, we're profitable, but we are not driven by revenue. We're driven by the quality of our work and the relationships that we have with our clients. That's what our employees crave. Yes, we need to make money and we need to be profitable in order to stay in business, but we are continually making decisions based on adding value to our clients and the quality of our work drives everything."

- **Jerry Mattys, CEO at Tactile Medical:** "I think it is a characteristic of good leaders to create a team where everyone thinks like the owner. And when I say that, I mean makes decisions where they understand the consequences of those decisions and understand the tradeoffs being made–short and long term, including profitability."

The Skeptic's Shift

By Paul Hillen

This isn't a topic where I really needed to make a shift. I had the good fortune of working for two very good, large, multi-national companies that were best-in-class in communicating the benefits of healthy profits to employees. At P&G, in addition to employees receiving an annual statement showing the company contribution to their profit-sharing account, each paycheck also showed the company contributions to their health care benefits and ESOP, programs that all exempt employees participated in. There was a clear line of sight and explanation to the profitability of the company.

At Cargill, it was very similar. Cargill showed each employee how better company profits contributed to a higher pension contribution. They also sent each employee a total compensation detailed report showing what each benefit component was and what percent of total compensation it represented. Employees saw how much the company was contributing to their overall well-being. In good profit years, the pension contribution was higher, and in lower earnings years it was lower. Again, there was a clear explanation and line of sight that, if the company did well, then employees benefitted.

I quickly realized, however, that my experiences with P&G and Cargill were not common. In discussions with friends at other companies, especially smaller ones, I found these practices of financial transparency were not common. In employer cases where there was not a profit-sharing program, pension fund, or even an ESOP, it was understandable that there was not an explanation. However, I was often surprised to hear how leadership did not even describe the contributions made by the company to employee benefits. In many of those cases, the employees would complain that they were not being paid enough, their bonus was not big enough, and that only senior management benefited from their hard work.

I think all of this could have been fixed by providing these employees with a semi-annual "total compensation report" showing employees how the company contributes to their total financial package including health-care premiums, 401(k), and other benefits. Additionally, it should be common practice to hold a biannual or quarterly meeting with employees, especially at small to mid-sized companies, explaining how healthy profits contribute to higher pay, higher benefit contributions, and longer-term job stability. Taking steps like these will lead to greater employee engagement and higher retention, because employees will see how the company cares about them.

Coaching Corner

How to Instill a Belief that Profits are Healthy for All

☑ **Develop a profitability training program for managers to use with employees:** Focus on the main keys to profitability that are role and level specific to help employees understand how their daily performance and decision-making directly impacts profitability. Help them understand the basics of a P&L statement, the key drivers of profitability, and how they can help grow it. Create programs to tie the ideas of profitability at work to increased personal financial literacy, in order to better manage their personal finances.

☑ **Review progress towards business profitability regularly (monthly or quarterly) with a public scorecard that helps employees learn how to recognize profitability:** Have managers make the connections for employees for how company profitability will enhance their own financial rewards. When paying profit-sharing, create a special payroll transaction outside the normal pay periods to highlight and celebrate the specific contributions.

☑ **Create an employee give-back budget, of both time and money, to encourage volunteer investments in community improvement:** An investment like this by management helps meet all of the Four Drives articulated by Kurt Nelson in this chapter. Monitor participation to ensure as many employees are involved in the community improvement efforts as possible. Increase the budget in times of greater-than-expected profitability.

☑ **BONUS:** Don't make the mistake of including financial incentive rewards with an auto-deposit connected to monthly salary. Give people real paper checks to celebrate their accomplishments–the intrinsic part of the reward is significantly diminished if you don't get to shake hands and say "good work!" The payroll team may see the extra work of producing checks as a hassle, but it's worth the extra effort.

CHAPTER 6
Goodness Pays Factor 3: Team-Based Culture

"Knowing when to be a leader and when to be a follower is the art of good leadership. The best leaders today understand that being a part of a high-performing team means, at some point, you're expected to step up and lead. And at other points, it's better to let somebody else lead. What that really means is the 'we' is more important than the 'me,' if you want to have a high-performing company."

Chris Policinski, retired CEO at Land O' Lakes

The Advent of "We is Greater Than Me"

Goodness pays when individual leaders step out of thinking: *"It's gotta be up to me,"* and instead embrace the idea that *nothing significant ever happens alone.* Most good leaders I've coached can point to a pivotal moment in their careers when they learned this lesson—sometimes after encountering a hard lesson, like Paul Hillen's example—that led to a "we is greater than me" orientation.

Here's why: stereotypical "great" leaders are portrayed in the movies and popular culture as bold people who, in the face of adversity, dig deep, find an extra gear, pull themselves up by their bootstraps, and will their way to win. Think of the Steve Jobs/Apple leadership story during the brink of Apple's near-bankruptcy in the late 1990s. When Jobs returned as CEO to the company which he had co-founded years before, he role-modeled a style of leadership that could be fittingly described as "superhero" leadership. After Jobs swooped in to save Apple from failure, he attracted great media and industry credit for achieving results no one else thought possible or could have done. Superhero leadership is an intoxicating notion, although exceptionally rare.

Today, we live and work in the age of leadership collaboration. The internet and mobile phone technology, which make gathering and sharing information instantly available to anyone, ushered in a new era of transparency where we expect a higher level of inclusion and fairness. People today generally reject the idea that any one person's leadership ability is somehow far superior to others, because we're less reliant than ever on others–including leaders–telling us what we need to do or know.

In the 1960s and '70s, CBS News anchorman Walter Cronkite, once dubbed "the most trusted man in America," regularly had 30 million viewers for his newscasts, which he always ended by commandingly saying: "And that's the way it is." Today, the evening newscasts of the "big three" networks–CBS, NBC and ABC–*collectively* don't attract 30 million viewers–even as the United States population has grown by 60% since the height of the Cronkite years. It's a fact that Americans don't need a Cronkite-style authority figure to tell them what's what anymore.

Goodness certainly requires courage and conviction, but goodness does not depend on any one individual leader's authoritative, heroic style anymore. That explains the importance of Goodness Pays Factor 3: Team-based culture. Creating a culture that rewards a "we is greater than me" approach, in which multiple people are accountable and rewarded for delivering on important promises, is crucial.

The Business Case for Team-Based Cultures

A "we is greater than me" orientation means that *all* participants–especially the leaders–believe teamwork is the best way to win together. Financially it makes sense, because strong teams reduce business risk with redundant follow-through systems and a strong bench of people who can backfill when needed. Those redundancies ensure the most important promises to customers, owners, and investors are kept and are accepted as the responsibility of the full team. Not just one superhero leader.

But most cost-cutting strategies in organizations inadvertently eliminate important redundancies. Recently, I was privy to an internal memo for a client. The CFO expressed her confidence that her cost-cutting efficiencies were going to improve the company's performance with this rationale:

> "Our confidence has never been higher, because we believe this re-organization and right-sizing trims our workforce down to the best and brightest–the people who always deliver. Our philosophy is to put the responsibility into the hands of people who seek accountability, and can handle the daily pressures...then our job is to get out of their way so everyone can succeed on their own merits. Again, our confidence has never been higher in our ability to execute."

What do you think happened? The memo was designed to motivate the company's self-proclaimed A-players. But the cost-cutting measures eliminated most of the supporting cast who helped the A-players deliver on their goals. Within a year of the memo, 60% of the best performers left the company. Most of those who left complained of a huge personal workload increase because their executive assistants were eliminated. Work that used to be done by internal sales and customer service people was now being done by the front-line sales people, after-hours on newly issued iPads. No wonder so many employees left.

The following research explains why the CFO's decision in the scenario above didn't work.

"Superchicken" Research: Collaboration, Not Superhero

In the 1990s, evolutionary biologist William Muir of Purdue University produced a series of animal experiments, popularly called the "Superchicken Research," which directly supports the idea that the highest-performing organizations *thrive together* rather than owe their performance to individual superheroes.

In seeking ways to improve the egg-producing productivity of chickens, Muir asked: Would the most productive egg-producing chickens, with specific breeding, produce a rare kind of "super-chicken" of top egg-producing offspring? It was a modern test of the underlying assumption of Darwin's "survival of the fittest" as a factor for success based on fierce competition.

Muir assembled and housed a flock of average egg-producing chickens, then he identified and separately housed a "superflock" of the highest egg-producing chickens. For each generation, Muir moved the most productive chickens from the average flock into the superflock. After six generations, he compared the two flocks. The results were astounding and maybe even counterintuitive.

The average flock chickens were plump, fully feathered, healthy, and more productive than ever. The superflock had only three chickens still left alive; they had pecked the other superchickens to death. As it turned out, the most productive superchickens were not superheroes but rather super-bullies. They achieved their productivity and superiority by suppressing the output of the other hens.

In the meantime, Muir found that the average chickens behaved in ways that protected the social and physical health of all the chickens in the cage. They created a nurturing environment for one another that resulted in significantly higher egg production for the "team" as a whole.

How Do Chickens Connect with Goodness?

To connect the superchicken insight to business, I turned to research by the Paris-based global business school INSEAD, whose MBA programs ranked at the top internationally by the *Financial Times* in 2016 and 2017. The school published its own research-based point of view about the power of collaborative leadership to explain how the school teaches its aspiring business leaders. INSEAD believes that treating one person on a team as a superhero with special powers and privileges lowers expectations for other employees. Because leaders who pin their hopes on a single performer are implicitly sending a message to their other employees: *You aren't good enough, your contributions don't matter as much as others, and you don't have a big part in shaping our future. That's for people above your pay grade.*

In research collected from those whom INSEAD described as "superhero" workers, we learn:

- One in four intended to leave their current employment within the year.

- One in three admitted to not putting all of his/her effort into the current job.

- One in five believed his/her personal aspirations were quite different from what the organization had planned for him/her.

You may think these behaviors of the "superhero" are counter-intuitive. If you've been told you are the best and you are the "chosen one" to lead us to better results, why would you then not put your best efforts into your job, and instead think about leaving when your future theoretically looks so promising?

The mistake in thinking about superheroes is that they are motivated by performance. The connection many leaders fail to make is that superheroes are primarily motivated by *their own* performance. They frequently aren't concerned with the fate of the larger organization, and they aren't even particularly loyal to the people who immediately surround them.

> The mistake in thinking about superheroes is that they are motivated by performance.

Because of this, and because they have been told they are the "chosen ones," the superheroes actually don't work as hard, and often look outside for other opportunities because they have been told they are exceptional. Additionally, it leads them to think that if they're already on top here, then maybe they can go elsewhere and do even better, often leading to an imminent job change.

So, is a workplace which is fueled by individual achievement and internal competition inherently bad? Not necessarily. Internal sales competitions, charitable fundraising challenges and employee award money for things like naming a new product or service often brings out the best in people. But the spirit of competition is difficult to sustain over the long term.

As Kurt Nelson at the Lantern Group explained in the prior chapter, the belief that internal competition among a team's strongest performers is the key ingredient for productivity is losing popularity among leadership experts. Instead, the leaders we interviewed gave greater credibility to the notion that the best, most sustainable results, come from collaborative team thinking.

"The key to our success has been building a creative group from four acquisitions over the past three years with people whose hearts are in the right places," said Lynn Casey, Chair at the public relations firm Padilla. "We had to find really talented people who have deep specialties, who also think 'team first.' That's not easy! We could easily fall into the temptation of letting the competition of really strong people within our different offices drive our growth. Instead, we are constantly working on the idea that when we work together for the benefit of our clients, we all win. That's what's working for us."

Why Pursuing Superhero Leaders is So Tempting

The economy goes up and down. Consumer behavior changes and competitive forces ebb and flow. Sometimes when all of these business factors are working against us, we start to think that a superhero leader could somehow, almost magically, turn things around.

In my role as a coach, I've been involved in many conversations in the executive offices of clients that start in one of the following ways:

- "We need a special sales and marketing leader with industry contacts to get us over the bar."

- "We need a business development person with a client list that will help us hit our targets."

- "We need to hire an R&D guru with the special expertise to leapfrog our competitors."

While any of these ideas could be true, it's risky thinking. Searching for the best talent is a good strategy. But sometimes in the recruiting process, we meet a candidate who makes us giddy with hope. We start to think things like *"If we could just get her, we'll soar!"*

Nearly every business owner and executive I know has a regretful story of trying to hit a home run by hiring a superhero leader. I've done it myself. It's exciting, because when we believe we have found the perfect person for the job, we get an intoxicating boost of positivity about the future. Often the mistake comes from a strong-willed leader who is hiring a person tied to one of his or her own lofty dreams, which is unlikely to come true. Especially when the dream is not fully embraced by the rest of the team.

The hidden danger of acquiring a superhero leader comes when we unintentionally send conflicting messages in the recruiting process. It's reasonable to recruit an exciting new leader by emphasizing how strong we believe the existing team is today. And it's also tempting to appeal to the ego of the candidate, communicating the message: "But we just can't seem to get the business to where we want it to be. What we really need is YOU to get us to the next level." With that, the candidate hears–rightly or wrongly–that she has been given the authority and autonomy to do whatever it takes, even if it wrecks your existing "strong team."

In that situation, it usually doesn't take long for a superhero leader to get short-term results but to also alienate other team members. The team begins to weaken when existing team members start to ask questions such as: "Is this the way we are going to win around here now?" Left unattended, underlying doubts about team cohesiveness can turn to bitterness and subversive behavior, which makes the *"thrive together"* idea impossible.

The negative consequences are even more obvious if the superhero doesn't generate quick business results. One leader we interviewed found a silver lining in one particular hiring failure:

"I hired a person who I thought was perfect to help us build a whole new competency that would put us on a whole new playing field," she said. "Initially, I was so excited about the possibilities– the national visibility and big new clients! But within a couple of months I was seeing warning signs in the team."

The team's performance began to falter as the new hire and existing team members failed to click with one another. Soon, a negative "we shall see" mood began to form around the team.

"Looking back, I let the struggle go on too long," she said. "I hung onto my dream in ways that made me temporarily blind, so I didn't intervene with coaching early enough. Then I had to endure the embarrassment of removing the very same leader I was so convinced would be a star. What I learned is how precious the team chemistry of trust and support is to our success."

The other scenario is that when you recruit a superhero leader with the bait that the existing team is strong and he/she is the missing piece; if that is not the case, you have set that leader up for failure. The story of a recent coaching client is a perfect example.

A marketing executive with a consistent history of strong business results was recruited by a company to lead its commercial efforts. He was initially told that he was the only missing link and that all of the other pieces were in place for the company to succeed. In less than three months, the executive realized the talent level in the other key positions was not as advertised. Determined to turn the ship around, he and the HR leader replaced more than half of the company's managers. It was distracting and very expensive to the business. Despite the company owners' permission to make these changes, they neither accepted any responsibility for exaggerating the strength of the company, nor changed their expectations for the company's growth and profitability. The executive's struggles to make this company work, despite its numerous problems, became too much, and he had no choice but to quit and find a new job. It was a hard lesson for both the owners and the marketing executive.

"Zero Cost of Candor" and Psychological Safety

The key ingredient to team thinking is being able to speak openly about any subject without suffering adverse consequences. It's an idea that former Cargill CEO Greg Page calls "zero cost of candor," and he believes it's an essential element to high performance–even when he's the target.

> The key ingredient to team thinking is being able to speak openly about any subject without suffering adverse consequences.

"To me, there was nothing more gratifying as a CEO than to be found wrong by my team," Page said. "How wonderful that is, right? It's the ultimate sign of a good team. Everybody learns something. The people on the team learn that sometimes they have better ideas than the CEO does. And the boss (me) learned that he has people around him who can fight into the second, third, and fourth innings on an issue without fear. We call that 'zero cost of candor.' It's alive when the whole team agrees that the organization wins when people on the team are comfortable enough to fight for what they believe in, without being afraid of negative consequences."

It's an idea that flourishes beyond Cargill. Google found that eliminating the negative costs of candor played an important part in its highest-performing teams. In 2017, Google released the findings of a long and intense study to determine how to create consistently high-performing teams for the thousands of projects it sponsors every year. The highly publicized study, called "Project Aristotle," was introduced in the August 2017 issue of *Harvard Business Review*. It asked the fundamental question: "Why do some teams excel while others fall behind?"

Google's research team included statisticians, engineers, and organizational and behavioral psychologists. Through more than 200 interviews, Google identified five specific characteristics, or unwritten rules, that keep its teams at optimal performance. The first four are predictable: *dependability*, which is getting things done to expectations; *structure and clarity*, which is about well-defined roles and goals; *meaning*, which is work that has personal significance for each of the team members; and *impact*, which is about how the purpose of the team impacts the greater good.

But it was Google's fifth identified characteristic which stood out and aligns with Page's "zero cost of candor" thinking. It's around the concept of *psychological safety*–which Google described as "*the belief that you won't be punished when you make a mistake.*" The author of the *Harvard Business Review* article, Laura DeLizonna, explained the findings this way: "Studies show that psychological safety allows for moderate risk-taking, speaking your mind, creativity, and sticking your neck out without fear of having it cut off–just the types of behaviors that lead to market breakthroughs."

Other research highlights the importance of psychological safety to team performance. To the points made earlier about the presence of a "superhero" on the team, it's likely that the superhero may alone feel that sense of psychological safety, emboldening the superhero's behavior. But when a whole team has that same degree of psychological safety, the team will confront the negative and/or destructive effects of a superhero leader. That's important because when teams have a high degree of psychological safety, the team becomes self-correcting–with or without the intervention of its leader. Team members can set their individual agendas and egos aside and work together to make mid-course corrections to ensure the full team hits its goals.

Rewarding "We is Greater than Me"

In keeping with the "we is greater than me" element of team-thinking, how does a leader transition from a traditional "hub and spoke" model, in which decisions and projects are handled along functional lines and rewarded individually, into one in which a team of those best suited for the project is formed and the team is rewarded for success? Transitioning to a new reward system is never easy. But if the business strategy is becoming more dependent on collaboration, high-performing teams will perform better if the incentives are more tied to "we" accomplishments than "me" accomplishments.

In working with executive teams striving to execute on bolder aspirations, we ask three simple questions to determine where and how such teams will need to create change in their systems.

Over the next three years:

1. Do we expect the requests from our customers to be less, or more complex?

2. Will those customers have less or more competitive choices?

3. Will the answers to the first two questions require less or more collaboration from us?

From these three questions, most, though not all, executive teams will conclude: We will have more complex requests from customers, and those customers will have more competitive choices, which will require more collaboration from us.

When executives answer these three questions in this pattern, the coaching strategy is then to move the client toward a more open system of planning, goal-setting, collaborating, and incentive-sharing to align with the changing requirements of the marketplace. Suddenly, it becomes a matter of how this team can begin to *thrive together*. Without making the shift to a more collaborative, open system approach to leadership, the team will falter or fail in its efforts to meet the future needs of its customers.

Nelson shared a specific example of how moving toward a team-based incentive system dramatically improved results at a pharmaceutical firm he was advising. The impetus for a new team-based reward system came from sales process re-engineering, which changed how pharmaceutical salespeople could involve more people on their teams, engaging with individual physicians. The firm moved away from its old, one-on-one sales strategy to a team-based approach with multiple sales team members interacting with the entire clinical team, including staff members, nurses, and physician assistants.

It was a big shift, because many of the firm's top performers were used to a superhero style of sales, achieving results through their own individual efforts. And they liked being compensated accordingly.

But the pharmaceutical company found that the shift to a "we" sales approach created a powerful urgency for all sales team members to perform at a higher level. Some of the top salespeople who felt strongly about the old model left the company.

But all of the remaining sales teams improved their performances, and the new top salespeople ended up earning even more money in the new model. In fact, everyone involved in the sales process made more money with the new team-based incentive system.

The shift from "me" to "we" was profitable for the pharmaceutical company because its team-based incentive plan was now aligned with its business strategy. "If the idea that profits are healthy for everyone is important to how goodness pays, then the most powerful incentives need to be aligned with team accomplishments," Nelson said.

> *The shift from "me" to "we" was profitable for the pharmaceutical company because its team-based incentive plan was now aligned with its business strategy.*

Making the Shift to "We"

Prior to publishing this book, I shared the success story in the preceding paragraphs with one of our firm's executive coaching clients, the CEO of a fast-growing, middle-market health care service provider. He reacted with this insight: "I just realized I didn't understand this concept until now. I've never had my direct reports share their individual goals, because I wanted them to be a little competitive with one another. I've just always believed that it's up to each person to hit her own goals, and that's how they could earn the most incentives."

Instead, what the CEO thought would be "healthy" competition turned out to be a self-inflicted damage. To make their individual year-end goals, the top leaders were making questionable decisions about resources that destabilized the business. It hurt the team's morale and called into question the integrity of the team's annual budgeting process.

The pharmaceutical company story was the catalyst for this CEO to adopt a full team-based incentive for the newly started fiscal year. Almost overnight, his team began working better together. The team finished that year ahead of plan, and 100% on strategy, because its members spent more time together and made business decisions together, without any of their prior dissension.

It is critical for teams to work together to achieve team-based rewards. Organizations that indicate they will reward on a team-based program, but then don't have their teams work together, risk lower performance because employees believe their own efforts won't be rewarded. Why? Because they cannot directly see or know if the other employees are pulling their weight.

The Human Dynamics Laboratory at the Massachusetts Institute of Technology (MIT) confirms what the health care services CEO learned with his change in incentives. Teams with shared incentives have 30% greater productivity. Why? Because these teams have more positive energy toward one another and engage in each other's success both inside and outside of formal meetings.

A similar study from the University of North Carolina showed that teams whose members simply got to know each other better achieved greater productivity. Increasing team familiarity by 50% led to a 30% decrease in budget deviations.

Intuitively, we know teams accomplish more than a collection of individuals. But the data is also clear: a "we" culture improves the bottom line. When leaders get the collective focus of the whole team toward the same goals, people start positively behaving in ways they didn't when they thought they were competing against each other.

"Nagging Rights" Can Be Healthy for Teams

The power of team performance also means a need for what we call "nagging rights"–a permission based, mutually negotiated set of shared commitments to help improve overall team performance. While "nagging rights" might sound like a negative, they carry a host of positive benefits in terms of encouraging partici- pants to achieve agreed upon group standards for accountability and encouragement.

> While "nagging rights" might sound like a negative, they carry a host of positive benefits

Former Harvard Business School professor and author David Maister first articulated the concept of using "nagging rights" in leadership and business in his book, *True Professionalism*. As Maister writes: "The best teams must willingly, knowingly, vol- untarily give someone else 'nagging rights' to keep them honest regarding chosen goals."

Nagging rights are not the same as nagging, which is an entirely different topic. Nagging rights work based on the idea that social pressure helps team members stay at their best. It's especially useful for encouraging others toward higher levels of performance–or reminding laggards that they need to pick up their performance. Anyone with a successful, long-term business relationship or a positive marriage knows the power of nagging rights.

For example, an executive will give nagging rights to his executive coach, or a mentor, to remind him to stick with a set of agreed-upon professional goals. At home, you might experience nagging rights if you ask your spouse to remind you about a goal, such as your diet or exercise regimen. The important thing to remember with nagging rights is that they must be freely given to another individual or group to enforce, and they must benefit all involved. Without this understood permission, nagging rights are simply just nagging.

Here's a good example of how nagging rights can work in action. A manufacturing firm unexpectedly lost an operational leader during a high volume production season. In response, the executive team created a shared commitment to have at least two executives join the shop-floor production meetings three times each day, at 9:00 a.m., 3:00 p.m., and midnight, seven days a week.

To make this happen, the executives had to negotiate who was going to be present at each meeting, for the good of the whole organization. It wasn't easy–especially for the midnight meeting attendees. But the executives kept themselves committed to the plan, via their internal nagging rights, and it worked!

Looking back on the experience, the team members collectively noticed that their leadership improved. The crisis caused them to create a shorter cycle of planning and problem solving.

And the executive team learned to be more intellectually honest in assessing the internal and external forces affecting their ability to produce results. "I think those four months were our finest hour as a team," the company's COO later commented. "We were decisive, fully present, honest, and really committed to the success of the whole enterprise."

I believe the best teams invest in themselves in much the same way–putting in the time necessary to establish shared commitments rather than creating rules that need to be policed by a supervisor. Leaders may wish to build a culture of nagging rights for three simple reasons:

1. The process of granting nagging rights within the team builds respect and trust, because everyone on the team needs to agree to accept "nagging" when he or she breaks the shared commitments.

2. Rather than depending on one superhero, a team with nagging rights honestly assesses situations, because they have psychological safety.

3. The team's goals are actually the "team's goals," with redundant follow-through systems to ensure the team wins or loses together.

Within this structure, who steps up and leads depends on the context–just as Chris Policinski observed in the opening quote of this chapter. In short, the concept of *thriving together* works if the team is tied together and rewarded with a "we" team incentive.

What Would Need To Be True?

Paul Hillen adopted the simple question: "What would need to be true?" when he was a brand manager at P&G and was having a hard time pinning down his leadership in making timely decisions. He often would do market research or analysis to support a key project he was advancing, only to be told that the decision-maker needed one more piece of information to make the decision. His frustration led him to create this key question: "What would need to be true for you to agree to move forward with this project and champion its market entry and success?"

Hillen started asking his managers, and especially the key decision-makers, "What would need to be true?" *before* he did any of the market research or analysis. This not only forced decision-makers to define the evidence they needed to determine a project's viability, but it also indicated the work required to gain approval. By having these specifications up-front, the process suddenly became more efficient, timely, and less expensive.

By asking "What would need to be true?" approval time for new projects was cut in half. As a result, Hillen and his brand team were more motivated because they knew they were working on the right analysis, and everyone was happier because they were consulted ahead of time on key project details. Getting this input up front led to a "personal contract" between the requestor and the brand team, leading to faster decision-making and a shared commitment to drive the project to success.

This example also highlights the importance of having a "we is greater than me" orientation because it takes into consideration the needs of senior management and the key people doing the work. It is tied to the Goodness Cornerstone of Promoting Fairness, as it is fair to all involved when team members know how a decision will be made and the amount and type of work required to properly inform this decision. What could be fairer than that?

More Team-Based Culture Insights

This chapter is the longest and most information-rich in our book because the leaders we interviewed spoke extensively about the importance of teams to their success. Within the following select quotations, you will see specific ways these leaders articulate the same message: "We is greater than me."

- **Marcia Page, Founding Partner and Executive Chair at Värde:** "I really don't like the term 'workplace cops,' because it implies we have to police each other by sticking to rules. What works best for us to be consistent is to agree on our role as ambassadors of the culture and the firm. That means we need to give permission to each other to call out the behaviors that don't fit. When we call each other out consistently, it becomes a virtuous cycle that repeats itself in ways that are good for all of us."

- **Mike McMahan, President at St. Francis Regional Medical Center:** "I have the most fun, and we get the best results, when my team is empowered to do their job and I get out of their way. We've agreed as a team that I'm here for removing the obstacles and to make sure there is honest, clear, and transparent communications at all times. When that happens we win together, and share in that success"

- **Liz Smith, President at Assurance Agency:** "I have found that getting buy-in from your team has the greatest impact on your success or failure as a leader. At one point, I started engaging in a "solo" leadership style with regards to some decisions that needed to be made. I quickly realized I needed the feedback from the team to be successful. They were very honest with me about the negative impact this had on them and then proceeded to provide feedback and several great ideas on how to maneuver the situation. This conversation turned the ship for us and everybody was very appreciative of the openness and dialogue."

- **Lynn Casey, Chair at Padilla:** "One of my colleagues calls our team culture the 'abundance' mentality, where you're not afraid to share credit. It means we're all in this together, and we don't have to waste energy looking over our backs. We're only human, so the self-motivated behaviors show up now and then...but the idea that you won't win at my expense wins out. Ultimately, the abundance mentality is how we thrive together."

The Skeptic's Shift

By Paul Hillen

I guess you could say I was "raised in the business world" on a hub and spoke mentality—the leaders set the agenda and gave direction, and others were expected to follow. Obviously, that model served both companies very well as they experienced strong growth in the 1980s, 1990s, and early 2000s, but that leadership model no longer really exists today.

When I transitioned to Cargill, the culture was more of a team-based, collaborative environment in which decisions and risk were routinely shared. This forced me to exercise different "leadership muscles." What had made me successful as a leader at P&G was now holding me back. I had the superhero mentality that I had to have all the answers, be well-prepared for every meeting, and set the strategy and direction at all times.

The 360 feedback exercise was a big wake-up call for me, and it worked. I was assigned an executive coach, Paul Batz, who helped me realize that all of the behaviors that were considered strengths at P&G were now derailing my career. With the help of my boss at the time, John Geisler, and our CEO, Greg Page, Paul Batz and I put together a plan to begin "exercising those new muscles." I made a complete shift from having all of the answers to collaborating with my peers and team members well ahead of the decision timeline. This resulted in far better engagement, followership, and results.

Coaching Corner

How Do You Build a Team-Based Culture?

☑ **Honest self-assessment:** Do you have an inner circle that is really operating like the "hub and spoke" system described in this chapter? If so, the small few who are in the inner circle likely experience much less risk when they are candid with you, while those outside the circle may not speak up. Consider hiring a coach or engaging your HR partner to stimulate conversations about how to create what Google calls *psychological safety* in your team. It may make sense to ask people "What are the unwritten rules of this team–both positive and negative–that we need to discuss?"

☑ **Nagging rights:** What recurring problems or weaknesses have become acceptable within the culture of your team to discuss, but fail to get corrective action? Make a list of those items, and negotiate shared commitments to ensure the team works on the problems until they are fixed. Finish the conversation by formally extending nagging rights, like how the manufacturing executives held each other accountable for attending the production meetings. Ask the whole team to call one another out when someone is stepping out of line, and encourage one another to stay focused on meeting the shared, negotiated commitments.

☑ **Audit team incentives for alignment with strategy:** Changing incentives evokes strong emotional reactions from people. Consider forming a sub-group of the leadership team to evaluate the alignment of executive incentives with the strategy and objectives to ensure the individual incentives are not undermining the collective motivations of the team. Consider the Four Drive Model as explained by Kurt Nelson in Chapter 5 as a structure to use for the audit.

CHAPTER 7
Goodness Pays Factor 4:
Timely and Transparent
Decision-making

"The CEO is fundamentally the agent of the owners. There are a lot of things in the job that can be described as 'leadership,' but the main thing is to make decisions that protect the financial and reputational health of the owners. If the owners aren't protected, the business can't survive. And if the business is not doing well, then it's limited in its ability to do good in the world, like employing people and giving back to the community."

Greg Page, retired CEO and Chair of Cargill

Decision-making in business is fundamentally about making daily progress toward accomplishing agreed-upon goals. When employees feel they continually have to wait for their leaders to make decisions that are important to their work, their progress slows, performance lags, and confidence erodes. In the data we collected, slow, ambiguous decision-making was highlighted as one of the biggest violations of *fairness* when people described poor leadership.

Three specific comments from the original Goodness Pays focus groups stimulated our interest in articulating the importance of decision-making as a factor for goodness in leadership:

- "I can handle a lot of pressure in my job–as long as I know why things above me in the organization are taking longer than what was promised. But when I don't understand the delays, I lose my patience and my frustration grows. That's just not fair to me or my team."

~ Senior Manager of Brand Management

- "What I appreciate most about my leader is how she keeps me informed, especially when there are internal negotiations that directly affect the timing of my project or impact my teams."

~ Vice President of Customer Service

- "I left my last job because nobody on the executive team felt empowered to make a decision without approval by the CEO and the board. We were constantly spinning on the simplest decisions, and our lack of speed hurt our results. Those same decisions get made in my current company by the managers, not the executives. That's why I like it so much better here."

~ Vice President of Research and Development

The learning here is that decision-making which gains employee respect is perceived to be both *timely* and *transparent*. Employees can be resilient, patient, and positive if they see decisions consistently get made and have a reasonable understanding of what's involved in that decision-making. So, good leaders eventually learn to be thoughtful, not only in communicating *what* they decide, but also *how* the decision was made. They also communicate when the decision will be made and adhere to that timing. This is especially important regarding decisions about people, which require extra care and attention to preserve a cultural sense of fairness and even-handedness.

Handling Pressure for Decision-Making Expediency

Consistently throughout our 15 interviews with senior executives, these leaders used many ways to describe what we are calling the "wisdom of aging" when it comes to leadership decision-making. It's the accumulated confidence that comes to leaders who have had both positive and negative experiences making important decisions. It's something that comes easier with more time spent in a leadership role.

"In PR and communications these days, our business is rapid-fire because many organizations today are held to a 24/7 need for stakeholder communication," said Lynn Casey, Chair at Padilla, whose firm advises CEOs on communication strategies related to important business issues. "I've learned that I'm at my best when I'm going slow to go fast."

What Casey is describing is how her personal experiences have taught her how to make the best decisions. Knowing when to go slow enough to really think through a strategic dilemma from every angle comes from self-assessing past experiences. The wisdom comes from intellectually honest self-assessment questions like:

- What big decisions have I made that turned out well for my organization, and why?

- What common elements are present in the decisions that haven't turned out well?

- What multiple sources of input and from where/whom do I need to be at my best?

"When I'm at my best, I am constantly thinking about the trends and sensitivities in our business, and I do that slowly and deliberately," Casey said. "Then I can use the benefit of that slow thinking to help our team form an opinion together–a common philosophy–so the individual practitioners can decide quickly by themselves in the moment for our clients."

When you're the one anxiously awaiting a leader's decision, it's easy to think that leaders are too slow to make decisions, and that faster is always better. While it's true that some organizations experience worse financial results because of slow or no leadership decision-making, simply deciding on things faster can make matters worse.

Daniel Kahneman, the Nobel Prize-winning economist and author of the best-selling book, *Thinking, Fast and Slow*, has a good handle on how people make effective decisions. His book examines what psychologists see as two separate mental systems we each have: fast thinking corresponds to what we might call "gut instinct"; slow thinking is based on deliberative reasoning.

> *Generally, fast thinking is more impulsive and emotional than what's involved with slow thinking;*

Generally, fast thinking is more impulsive and emotional than what's involved with slow thinking; fast thinking typically leads more to a reaction than an actual decision.

According to Kahneman, we are usually better off when we carefully make slow thinking decisions. The problem with fast thinking choices is that unless they're within our area of expertise–for example, a brain surgeon in the midst of surgery–there are likely too many variables and too much volatility to result in the right decision. Think of stock investors who buy shares based on a "hunch" or a "good feeling." Similarly, business leaders who think they can regularly make big decisions quickly and accurately each time are substituting confidence for sound reasoning. That doesn't stop leaders from making rash decisions, however.

David Donnay, PhD, President of SKS Consulting Group, a management consulting firm, isn't surprised by overly fast executive decision-making. His organization has been advising organizations on leadership and talent decisions for more than 40 years. "Executives, in general, have an inherent bias for action," Donnay said. "The speed of the Internet–particularly social media–has enabled both problems and opportunities to rise to a level of perceived panic very quickly. When executives give into their inherent bias for action, this fast decision-making often creates negative consequences, sometimes described as 'knee jerk.'"

What's important in this learning is the need for leaders to check their need for speed. Unless the news media or investors are standing right outside your door demanding an immediate answer to an urgent question, sometimes the classic "let's sleep on this" decision-making instinct is a good self-correcting behavior. Making quiet time to ponder, think, and take in other perspectives helps executives avoid making a "bias for action" mistake in the heat of the moment. It can be especially helpful when leaders tell others why they are taking time to think through something important.

"I believe the most valuable question a senior executive can ask when under the pressure to make a decision is: Why is a decision necessary *right now?*" Donnay said. "The wisdom of good leadership comes in considering the potential consequences. Could making a decision right now for one customer, vendor, or employee, jeopardize our relationship with other customers, vendors, or employees in the future?"

Ambiguity Can Be Problematic

The pressure for rapid decision-making can sometimes come from within our own organizations, such as when individual contributors want fast decisions so that they can react quickly to prove their worth in the company. Leaders at every level can easily imagine this picture: There's a line of employees standing outside your office door–or waiting for a return phone call–and they all think they need a decision about something *right now.*

"Many employees tend to have a singular focus; they want to follow the rules and check things off their list," Donnay said. "When we become managers, we find we need to focus on the success of others, and that increases the complexity of our jobs. When we become leaders, our focus needs to turn to the success of our enterprise, and that multiplies the trade offs associated with ambiguous problems where there aren't easy answers."

Some young leaders have been given a high level of judgment opportunities, despite very few years of life experiences. But often these leaders lack a quality perspective on how to deal with inherent decision-making tensions because they simply haven't experienced enough decision-making dilemmas.

For example, there's the young CEO I once coached on his decision-making as he was dealing with a lapse in employee judgment. The dilemma was sparked by the company's universally common customer service mantra *"The customer is always right."*

Thinking that pleasing the customer was their company's top priority, several young service managers at this CEO's company had allowed themselves to be pressured into lowering prices for a top customer. When word got out that this top customer had negotiated a better deal, it started an avalanche of inquiries from other customers demanding the same new deal–which would deal a major financial blow to the organization. Unwittingly, these service managers had put the company's entire value proposition in jeopardy.

The young CEO admitted that his first instinct upon hearing this news was to yell and scream: "How could anyone let this happen?" He wanted to make a statement to all employees by firing the service managers involved. Instead, he chose to take my advice and sleep on the dilemma.

In the calm of the morning, he saw the inherent tension with his employees unwaveringly following the mantra *"The customer is always right."* It's a quippy phrase that sounds good. But it's not really true. The intention is to get employees focused on the customer, but no business can survive if customers *always* get what they want, especially when their demands include unsustainable pricing.

Instead of berating or firing his overly generous managers, the CEO decided to help his team develop a deeper, shared understanding of *"The customer is always right."* He also began a new empowerment training program for front line managers. "Our intent was for our pricing and core program to be good for both the customer and the company, but I hadn't prepared our people to think this way," the CEO admitted. "The problem was on me."

Donnay explained what happened from an organizational psychologist's perspective: "For most employees, ambiguity doesn't feel good. So they would rather interpret simple principles like: *"The customer is always right,"* into meaning, the customers always gets what the customer wants. It's easier to follow that rule." What worked with the CEO's approach in the story above is that he processed his decision from multiple perspectives, saw how and where he needed to step in, and was transparent in communicating the "why" behind his thinking and decision-making.

What Do Quality Decision-Makers Have In Common?

"The best decision-makers have a process," Donnay explained. "They create a discipline to consider both the patterns of the past, and the vision for the future. And that process usually involves a team."

The best decision-makers have a process,"

To get to that level of decision-making, Donnay recommends assembling a team equally balanced by what he calls "rear view mirror" and "windshield" type thinkers. The rear view mirror perspective is based on facts and past occurrences, which reveal a pattern of where you are today. However, while fact-based patterns are important, they are not always projectable into the future. Thus, you also need windshield thinkers who can provide a future vision of how things can be. Individually, these two types of thinking are incomplete. Combined, they are complementary.

Because most leaders already have both a past and future perspective, and a bias toward using one or the other, improving a leader's decision-making is more about embracing the idea: *"It's not about me."* Or, in other words, having leaders believe: *"I may not necessarily be the expert on this topic, which is why I've surrounded myself with talented and intelligent colleagues who can provide their perspective when asked."* Good decision-making is an others-centric thought process. It takes practice.

One way that leaders can improve their decision-making is by joining an executive peer group or seeking out a coach. Both options provide a structure for reflection and a predictable cadence to discuss the positive or negative consequences of their decision-making.

Good decision-making is an others-centric thought process. It takes practice.

"Just knowing I will have the opportunity to review my decision-making with my coach helps me think deeper about what I'm doing," said a hospital CEO, as she reflected on her development. She was challenged with a significant task: Improve patient care quality and safety at the hospital by collaborating with her administrative and clinical staff.

"In the hospital setting, it's easy to align with either the administrative or clinical side of any problem. My previous orientation was to make decisions from the administrative side of any disagreement," she recalled. But from the CEO perspective, getting hospital staff members to embrace quality and safety improvements required a balanced perspective. And when the issues involve life or death consequences, staff members are often reticent about speaking out for fear of getting someone else in trouble.

Knowing this context, the hospital's CEO decided to improve her team's performance by emphasizing to employees the importance of speaking up rather than tightening down the rules, and issuing penalties for breaking those rules. She made the shift in thinking by seeking out the opinions of others–both peers and her coach–to decide on her approach. By celebrating "speaking up" she reduced the fear of negative consequences (similar to Page's "zero cost of candor.") In fact, as employees were rewarded for speaking up, the number of critical incidents went down. In three years, the hospital rose from the bottom third among its peer group for patient care quality and safety into the top 10th percentile.

Why Transparency Matters

Most people can put up with a lot of uncertainty if they feel well-informed. It's when the flow of communication stops that people get worried and teams are tested to their limits.

The senior leaders of a private, equity owned company had been counting on a change in ownership for nearly two years. With every passing day, tensions rose, because dialogue between the company's owners and management team had mysteriously gone silent. For some unknown reason, information about the company's pending sale was suddenly off limits. Was the sale still going to happen? What did this mean for the future of the business? Were employees still going to remain with the company? Absent any information to the contrary, it's easy for employees' minds to endlessly speculate about things, especially when the issues begin to affect them personally.

What couldn't be immediately communicated to senior leaders was that negotiations for the pending sale were going badly, threatening the completion of the deal. These were things that the CEO couldn't talk about. Yet the CEO also knew he had to quickly improve his communication transparency because he was losing the hearts and minds of the people he had worked so hard to recruit. He called for my firm's coaching help when two of his key people told him that they were pursuing new jobs outside the company.

We recommended a facilitated exercise called "Momentum Analysis" to help the company's leaders think about their situation through the lens of other people–an important factor in good leadership decision-making. The CEO and his senior leaders analyzed the positive and negative momentum in their situation through both an internal and external perspective. The most obvious source of negative momentum internally was the fact that the CEO couldn't talk about the current negotiations.

So, with that information on the table, what happened next was surprising. The team unanimously agreed to take it upon themselves to find a new owner who would invest in their strategy. With the right buyer, everyone could win, including the existing board.

"That exercise changed everything for me," exclaimed one of the vice presidents who had been planning to leave. "I was so impressed with how open, honest, and sometimes raw our discussion was. Our CEO created a lot of respect in the room because he was willing to engage us in his most difficult leadership dilemma."

In less than 100 days, the CEO found a new owner for the company, and the sale was completed in time to preserve a valuable service contract with the company's largest customer.

"What I learned is the importance of transparency for maintaining the morale and confidence of our team," the CEO said. "Until that off-site meeting, I was carrying all the weight of the situation on my shoulders and that was just making things worse. When I recruited my senior leaders, I promised an opportunity to be involved in leading a growth company–the good, bad, and the ugly. But somehow, I thought I needed to protect them from the ugly part. I was wrong, because they really needed to be involved with me in working through the ugly part."

Liz Smith, President at Assurance Agency, offered similar insight to what this CEO had learned: "If you make a good-faith effort to make decisions that are best for your employees and the company, it will ultimately pay off. If a wrong decision is made, learn from it. Without finger-pointing or blame. Good leaders gain credibility and gain the respect of employees by acknowledging their failures or bad decisions. People are going to believe in you and they're going to want to follow you if you are transparent in your decision-making."

What we can learn from these examples is how transparency in decision-making can be even more important than timeliness, because most high-performing cultures today are driven by the spirit of collaboration. So when a leader makes an important decision in isolation, those affected by the decision feel unfairly excluded. And when the sense of unfairness festers, it can turn into bitterness and a loss of trust.

Discussion Models Prompt Healthy Dialogue

A simple way to draw out the perspectives of team members on important decisions and avoid isolated decision-making is to use a discussion tool. The Momentum Analysis tool below helps leaders consider a collective of perspectives when making decisions. Here's how it works: with a team or a thought-partner, state a specific goal related to an important decision you are making. Begin by discussing the "internal forces of positive momentum" in motion to achieve the goal–writing your collective thoughts in the upper left box on the tool, labeled #1. "Internal" means inside your company, "external" means outside, which typically means community, industry, competitors, etc. Continue with the same process moving clockwise through #4. Consider both the amount and significance of the data in each box to contribute to your decision-making.

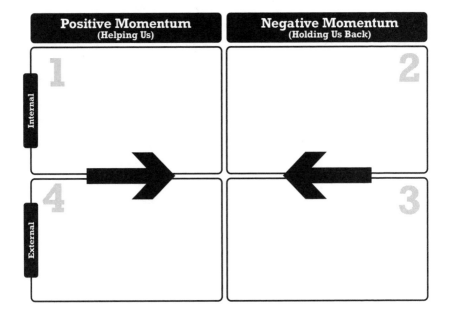

Decisions are Both Intellectual and Emotional

Good leaders can gather and weave together a wide variety of information, including data, the opinions of others, trends, predictions, and the emotional context of the situation. When you involve others in this process, both the information-gathering and the actual decision-making process becomes about building trust and community confidence in the decisions being made. When important items go unexplained, there's likely to be trouble.

"Nothing gets people more upset than when someone else makes an unexplained decision that negatively affects their process or results," Donnay said. One leader who thoroughly understands this degree of clarity and transparency in her decision-making is Marcia Page, Founding Partner and Executive Chair at Värde, a 25-year-old global private investment firm focused on finding undervalued investment opportunities on behalf of clients, such as pension funds, insurance companies, and affluent families. As Page explains, Värde is all about prudent decision-making, which is both timely and transparent.

"We work in a business where our employees constantly make decisions using other people's money," Page said. "Transparency has been a key ingredient to building trust, growing our business, and setting our firm apart."

At the outset, one of Värde's core commitments was to be completely transparent with the company's investors and employees. "In the early days of our industry, that was not the case for most kinds of hedge fund models," Page said. "It was our 'secret sauce' when many other firms like ours were saying: 'Well, just trust us' My response to that was, 'What? That makes no sense!' Our clients need timely and relevant information about what we are doing and why. That's good business, and that's what they deserve."

Transparency is the oxygen of Värde's business because employees, with many levels of responsibility, are making decisions with clients' money. The firm's website lets everyone know that its investments are based on complexity and risk. So, Värde, in turn, needs employees who are equally drawn to its transparent, investment-driven, risk management strategy. That's why the firm has an ultra-careful hiring process, checking candidates for their potential fit within the Värde culture, as well as technical talent. It's a strategic move which is not the norm in the "alternative asset" sector of the investment industry. Yet Page wouldn't have it any other way.

"Every one of our employees needs to be comfortable with describing what they're doing with our clients' money," Page said. "The more our clients understand what we're doing, the more they can appreciate how we help them make money. We can't do business any other way than being transparent in this manner."

Decisions Always Carry Risk

Transparency is one strategy to help to drive out risk in decision-making, but there are others. Good leaders also know how the perception of risk increases fear in individual decision-making. In Chapter 6, you read how Google values *psychological safety* as a way to ensure employees won't feel punished for speaking up or making a mistake. That same concept applies to this discussion about decision-making. It's why good leaders avoid describing daily business situations with emotional words like "difficult," "complicated," "significant," or "important," because they unnecessarily increase the natural fear already present in decision-making.

> Good leaders avoid describing daily business situations with emotional words like "difficult."

"In business, the stakes are high if something goes wrong because of a decision. So naturally, there is some risk," Donnay said. "I like to teach leaders to think of decision-making like a professional golfer. Golfers regularly hit tee shots to start playing any given golf hole. Fear only creeps into the equation when the golfer–or a caddy or commentator–uses the word 'important' to describe that particular shot. In reality, it's just another shot. The words 'important' or 'dangerous,' combined with the elevated consequences of winning or losing, increases the pressure because of the implication of inflated risk. It's better to treat decisions consistently and prepare to learn from the outcomes, good or otherwise."

Growing any business is about accepting and understanding your own thoughts and feelings toward risk. Leaders who invest the time to know their risk tolerance, and how their colleagues accept risk, will lessen the personal stress of decision-making. The best decisions happen when the perspectives of all of the people around the executive team table are considered.

Chris Policinski, retired CEO at Land O'Lakes, looked at the context of risk from his more than 30 years of management experience in the highly competitive, tight margin food industry. "Growth means doing something different than you have been doing. That means taking a risk," he said. "Being comfortable with risk means exposure to failure. A large piece of my job was engaging people in understanding risk in a constructive way, changing the language from 'We're failing' to 'That's just learning.' What did we learn and how are we going to go forward? We can't get into the habit of thinking so small that we drive out all of the risk. And we can't wait on higher-risk situations for so long that the downside becomes more painful than it needs to be."

The key learning here is to avoid labeling decisions as "bad" or "failures." Sometimes that's hard to do, especially when we are emotionally connected to the outcomes. But when a team provides input into a higher-risk decision, the consequences–whatever they may be–can also be shared to lessen the fear that may be present.

For instance, the promise that athletes and soldiers make to their colleagues, "I got your back," is a unifying, confidence building commitment that helps instill confidence and turns the fear of failure into a learning experience.

Ray Kowalik, CEO at Burns & McDonnell, thrives on the learning power of candid decision-making. "The markets move so fast today, so we need to use our base of experience to make timely decisions without fear," he explained. "We've made some mistakes, and we've lost some business we really wanted, and some people were really disappointed. The only choice we have is to accept mistakes as part of the learning process. If we get better because of it, then it's worth it. And if we don't get better, then we have a real problem. A really important part of our success is the open process of sharing our learning from both wins and mistakes broadly with people so that we can all get better."

Employees gain confidence and give respect when their mistakes are legitimately perceived as important learnings, instead of career-threatening. The underlying value here is fairness–if one person gets to "learn" from the mistakes, and others get punished, goodness vanishes.

Decisions about People Are Especially Important

It's been said that the CEO is only as good as his or her team. So, aspiring to hire only the best and brightest seems like a good strategy. But there are countless examples of how sports teams don't win championships by having all superstars on the team. That's also true in business. Jim Collins, in his book, *Good to Great*, smartly offered up the idea that good leaders start with the idea of "who" is on the team before they commit to bold deadlines for specific accomplishments. He coined the idea of getting "the right people in the right seats on the bus," which aligns neatly with the concept that goodness pays.

However, two time-sensitive temptations impair decision-making about people: first, the need to fill a position quickly; and second, a self-imposed pressure to decide alone. Both temptations can be overcome by staying true to the factor of being "timely and transparent" in your talent decisions.

There are countless examples of how sports teams don't win championships by having all superstars on the team.

"This goes back to my comment earlier about the executive's bias for action," Donnay said. "When one person gets too excited about one candidate and moves too quickly, that's a very common hiring mistake."

The management adage "hire slowly and fire quickly" seems to go in and out of favor with each generation. Tech companies with a voracious appetite for talent seem to operate with a hire quickly, fire quickly mentality. It's supported by the entrepreneurial mantra, *fail quickly*. But while that idea is good for product development, it's not aligned with goodness when applied to people. Who among us hasn't worked with someone who was hired too quickly and proved to be a "train wreck" on the job? Who wants to go through that kind of experience again?

A good guide to manage any anxiety associated with a talent search that's taking longer than expected is to ask the question: "What's the rush?" Good leaders know that the mistakes of making a bad hire too quickly can be more damaging than a slow search process. A good team can function with an open seat at the table, especially when the team members are emotionally invested in doing what's right for the business. In fact, for some, learning to fill the talent void can be an important development opportunity to learn new skills and experience parts of the business they might not otherwise see.

More Timely and Transparent Decision-Making Insights

The theme of timely and transparent decision-making was informed by multiple perspectives in our interviews, some of which are highlighted in these direct quotes:

- **Greg Page, retired CEO and Chair at Cargill:** "You could write a whole book on fairness and leadership. Someone is always going to be upset about certain decisions. I always ask people if they press me, do they want to be treated equally or fairly? The right answer is 'fairly.' You'd be surprised how many don't say that."

- **Colleen Needles Steward, CEO at Tremendous! Entertainment:** "When I'm at my worst as a leader, I know I'm slow to respond, and I tend to make mistakes because I don't move on things in a timely manner. When I'm at my best I'm fully present in the moment, and my thinking is clear...I'm less reactive and much more decisive."

- **Clara Shih, CEO at Hearsay Systems:** "When business is good, I freely let others get involved in decision-making. But during rough times, I learned to lead from the front, to be visible during those tough times. For me, that means being the one who is visibly accountable, leading by example in making the tough calls that need to be made."

- **Lynn Casey, Chair at Padilla:** "Our business is a people business, so the dynamics of managing strong, emotive people is sometimes daunting. That's why some of our most important decisions are about who is on any given team for our clients. People decisions are difficult."

- **Chris Policinski, retired CEO at Land O'Lakes:** "When we would have somebody on our team who didn't work out, I looked at that as my failure. It's both a selection failure, and a coaching failure by me, for not providing the right feedback along the way. It takes good coaching skills to say in the moment: 'When you did that, the consequences weren't good. Let's figure out how you can do that differently so it's better for all of us.' Deciding not to coach is a decision to let someone on your team fail."

The Skeptic's Shift

By Paul Hillen

"It's like racing a Porsche, you have to go slow to go fast." Those were the words from my executive coach, Paul Batz. That is when I made the shift. My natural inclination is to make decisions quickly so I can move on to the next one. As I mentioned in a previous chapter, I also have a disposition to make sure I have thought through all the possibilities and present them to our team so we can move quickly with our go-to-market plans.

While I've never owned a Porsche or even driven one–much less raced one, once I understood Batz's analogy it made perfect sense relative to my natural decision-making approach. To avoid the car losing traction, you have to drive slower going into a turn, and accelerate out of the turn. If the Porsche driver accelerates into the turn, there is a good chance the car will fishtail and crash.

The analogy to decision-making is that leaders need to bring others along with them. In my case, instead of making the decision or developing the plan and then getting others to agree to it, I needed to seek their input up front and develop the plan with them. Then, as people began to see where the plan was going (the wheels straighten out), the leader could go fast in the execution because, like the wheels, they were in full alignment.

It was counter to how I had learned to do things at P&G, where having your thinking developed and your plan thought through before engaging others was critical for speed. However, once I applied it at Cargill, it worked great. I actually believe I increased the speed of decision-making because people were a part of the plan and when they started to get excited about the possibility, they started saying "When can we get started?" instead of "Why should we do this?"

Coaching Corner

How to Make More Timely and Transparent Decisions

☑ **Reflection for improvement–data or vision?** Think back on some of the best decisions you've been involved with, and some of the decisions that didn't work out the way you hoped. Write down at least three examples for both. What was the influence of "rear view mirror" data-oriented thinking? What was the influence of "windshield" vision-oriented thinking? What was the outcome if you did not use one or either of these decision-making approaches? Use the learning from both outcome categories to create a specific process for decision-making going forward.

☑ **Self-assessment:** What types of decisions bring out fear or hesitancy in you? Are they fast decisions, or decisions with large financial implications–or both? Share your insights with your team, and discuss how a more collaborative approach with people who have complementary strengths can reduce your fear or hesitancy.

☑ **Hiring review:** Engage your team in an intellectually honest assessment of their hiring patterns over their careers. What did the hiring mistakes have in common? What made the hiring successes work out? Create a process with shared commitments to improve both speed and confidence for future hiring.

☑ **Bringing others along:** Look back at some projects where you had people in the organization who struggled to get on board with your plan. What could you have done differently? Could you have gone slower up-front and eventually increased speed in the decision-making and execution phases?

CHAPTER 8
Goodness Pays Factor 5:
Magnetic Ethics

"I believe to my core that ethical business has always been good business. It's a commitment to keep the business healthy for the others who come after you. Organizations that have endured the test of time, in their DNA is this long-term, ethical point of view. Good leaders figure out how to stay true to that DNA, while also meeting the challenges of short-term performance objectives."

Chris Policinski, retired CEO at Land O'Lakes

How High Ethics Fosters Goodness

Good leadership is about creating great results with a team of people in ways which could not be accomplished by working alone. The most sustainable results happen when people *thrive together* through a culture of encouragement, accountability, and good teamwork.

Throughout the research for this book, it became clear that people are attracted to leaders who demonstrate they are ethical in how they produce business results. And people pull away from those who are not. Every one of the 15 leaders we interviewed for this book talked about doing the right things in the eyes of the people most important to their success–family, friends, colleagues, customers, and investors. That's no coincidence; we chose these leaders based on their positive business reputations.

The allure of "great results" alone is not enough. From the verbatim comments in the 900-person quantitative survey, we repeatedly read that leaders who are lacking in ethics have a difficult challenge in keeping the trust of high-caliber talent long enough to build a business fueled by goodness. This data caused our lead researcher, Jeri Meola, to emphatically state: "Without ethics, the idea that goodness pays is dead."

"Without ethics, the idea that goodness pays is dead."

What is Business Ethics?

For purposes of this chapter and book, I define business ethics as: *a system of moral principles, based on the governing laws and policies of the company, which determine how people make decisions both personally and professionally.* Leaders make decisions every day from their interpretation of what's "right" or "wrong." The best leaders consistently make the time to ensure managers and employees are part of that interpretation, whether anyone is watching or not. And they use the same ethical principles in their professional lives that they apply in their personal lives.

Clara Shih, CEO at Hearsay Systems, articulated the connection between ethical business and goodness straight-on: "Like goodness pays, bad behavior also gets back to you. If you're getting great financial results, but you're behaving like a jerk, no one will want to work with you twice. Conversely, if you're a good leader who is a good person, who's getting those same results, then everybody will want to work with you again."

The Perspective of Others

John Dalla Costa is one of the strongest voices on ethics in business. He's the founder of the Center for Ethical Organizations, based in Toronto, Canada. In his book, *The Ethical Imperative,* he articulated the simple ethical axiom "ethics is others." It's not about deflecting our behaviors onto others. It's about using the viewpoint of others as a tight filter to determine what is and what is not acceptable.

Dalla Costa explains how there can be substantial ethical tensions that any one individual can reason away in her solitary mind. The simplest daily ethical dilemmas for employees include whether or not to use a business expense account for personal gain or convenience, and assessing when it's OK to use business supplies like paper and pens, printers, copiers, or mobile phone minutes for personal reasons.

Technically, ethical breaches like these can be labeled as stealing. And if these same ethical breaches involve a lot of money, it can rise to the level of embezzlement. Dalla Costa suggests the best strategy to avoid even the smallest ethical mistakes is for leaders to surround themselves with a circle of like-minded leaders who are competent thought partners to help determine the right ethical choices.

Executive leaders experience more complex ethical issues, such as determining when confidential information is best shared to protect an employee, or the interests of a customer. Or, understanding important conflict of interest laws/agreements which require disclosure of specific information to preserve the trust of analysts, investors, and employees. Informed leaders today should have a heightened sense of awareness about ethical issues, because it seems as if *The Wall Street Journal* and *The New York Times* have regular stories about ethical lapses, such as price-fixing, insider trading, or breaches of non-disclosure agreements.

Leaders with aggressive career aspirations create an unavoidable ethical quandary as they consider new job offers in other companies, while they are still working in their existing job. It's a common balancing act, not unlike keeping one foot on each side of a railroad track. One foot is on the side aligned with personal growth and opportunity. The other on the side of meeting the expectations of the current employer. Ethical leaders behave in ways aligned with the best interest of both the current employer, and also based on their sense of responsibility to family and larger career aspirations.

I believe the key to handling small and large ethical quandaries is involving other highly ethical leaders in assessing ethical dilemmas, to reduce the risk of making the wrong choices. What I like most about Dalla Costa's perspective is the idea that the strongest ethical compass comes from "an aspirational intention to serve other people, more than we serve ourselves." I've used that lens in my coaching and clients really find it powerful.

The Benefit of Ethics: Magnetism

From a bottom-line perspective, it's in your best business interest to foster an ethical culture. By operating ethically, you'll more likely attract the best employees and the best customers who are interested in trusting in and associating with you because of your values. As multiple studies have shown, you will also likely produce greater profits, higher shareholder value, and lower operational costs and risks.

"Our biggest calling card in the industry is the caliber of people who work for us," said Colleen Needles Steward, CEO at Tremendous! Entertainment. Her firm has grown more than 500% over the past five years by producing wholesome, educational programming with talent who had previously been accustomed to working in the ethically challenged trades of Hollywood.

"We have been able to attract more and more talented people who walk the walk and who really insist that things be done in a reputable way," Needles Steward said. "We've created a great reputation with great people. The people influence the quality of our product, which also influences who wants to do business with us, and who wants to partner with us on new projects."

As both Shih and Needles Steward have shared, the foundation of ethical leadership in their companies attracts both good talent and good business. Our research identified three distinct practices which make ethics a magnetic business quality:

1. Articulating ethical standards for behavior, based on enduring values.

2. Role modeling how those standards are to be followed.

3. Treating employees as people first in order to attract good people.

These three practices are more than just in-business moral choices. Wise business owners and leaders have taken notice that the world is literally watching them. Today, there are nearly 2.5 billion people worldwide with smartphones who can share their owner's sentiments about *anything,* at any time. For some smartphone users, that can mean recording and broadcasting any perceived mistake, misstatement, or unusual behavior by a leader in their workplace. Retired Cargill CEO and Chair, Greg Page, had a phrase he used often in communicating to employees the company's guiding principles and values: "In a world where you can't hide anything, you better have nothing to hide".

"Over the course of my career, the most obvious change in business today is that anything you do is going to be available for viewing by the world outside your own walls," said Jerry Mattys,

CEO at Tactile Medical. "If you aren't an ethical leader, you won't survive, let alone thrive."

High Standards Based on Values

What's required in leaders today is a constant sense of inner integrity. Page provided his personal point of view on the subject: "What I'm most proud of in my tenure as CEO of Cargill is that, through it all, I didn't do anything to embarrass my mother. Whether your thought process comes from the Hippocratic Oath in medicine, *'First do no harm,'* or something similar, at some level, the main motivator needs to be to meet the expectations of somebody who you hold in high regard. For me, that was my mother."

What Page is explaining is his way of articulating Dalla Cosa's axiom, "ethics is others." As Page explained, there are many ways that unethical behavior can be communicated: "At some point all leaders need to accept an attitude of disclosure. It's facing the fact that we live and work in a world that is a glass house, where others can see basically everything you are doing. It's a place where nothing can be hidden, and everything can be shared in an instant. We need to act accordingly, all of the time."

Richard Davis' "grandmother clause" and Page's "didn't do anything to embarrass my mother" integrity statements are ethical frameworks based on family values–a powerful motivational force shared by most cultures. Yet not everyone, for whatever personal reasons, feels the positive influence of a family member as an inspirational source for their ethical behavior. So what then?

Some of the most ethical leaders I know have learned what *not to do* from leaders who set bad examples. And their determination to never repeat those mistakes became a powerful motivating force. From one of the book interviews: "The culture in the company where I started my career was built on the idea that the leaders one or two levels up in the organization would openly take credit for the ideas generated by the younger team members. For a short while, I actually thought that's how things work in the business world," she exclaimed. "When I left to start my own firm, I vowed to never devalue the contributions of my employees, because of how bad that made me feel."

Sometimes the most powerful learning is learning what not to do.

When I start new coaching engagements, I hear this same theme over and over again–sometimes the most powerful learning is learning what *not to do* from being on the receiving end of bad or inappropriate leadership behaviors.

Role-Modeling High Ethical Standards

One of the most common ways that companies lapse into ethical misconduct is when senior executives–or even a prominent single executive–begin to behave in ways that are ethically inappropriate and other employees take note and begin to act similarly. The thinking becomes some variant of: "Hey, if 'the boss' can do it, why can't I?" That's how you can eventually get a massive business scandal, such as the one which led to the bankruptcy and elimination of the Enron Corporation, once the nation's fifth-largest corporation, and it led to the de facto dissolution of Arthur Andersen, once one of the five largest audit and accountancy partnerships in the world. Too many top executives take their "ethical cues" from ethically challenged colleagues and clients.

By contrast, business leaders who have high standards for ethics, and ensure that they only hire and employ similarly ethically strong employees, serve as ethical role models for their employees. Such leaders make sure that everyone knows and adheres to a defined, written standard of conduct. By so firmly advocating and demonstrating ethical behavior, leaders create a strong ethical work culture, which becomes both common practice and self-policing, with "bad seeds" quickly weeded out.

That's the kind of ethical work culture that Umit Nasifoglu, President at Wedding Day Diamonds, sought to build when he and his brother began their jewelry business. Nasifoglu knew up front the inherent challenges in his line of work. "We are in the jewelry business, an industry that's really difficult for customers to know if they get what they pay for," he said. "So, our ethics are probably our most valuable strength. I don't know any other way. Goodness, to me, starts with being ethical and honest with our employees, so that they can be that way with our customers also. It's about treating other people consistently with the ethics you want to instill in your company. When our employees experience that, they pass it on to our customers."

The success of a jewelry business–or any business–is about creating a magnetic pull where customers want to come back again and again over a long period of time. That's consistent with Chris Policinski's perspective in the signature quote of this chapter. To make his point, Policinski pointed out a sensational and simple example of how short-term thinking proved damaging to banking giant Wells Fargo, and how questionable ethics of the bank's leadership hurt customer retention.

In 2016, Wells Fargo suffered an embarrassing breach of public trust when consumer advocacy groups revealed that bankers at some of the bank's local branches had been opening up accounts for customers without their permission. Why would these bankers do this? Banking experts surmised that Wells Fargo's sales incentives caused some managers to secretly open these phony accounts to hit the bank's short-term sales goals. When the world learned about this, the reputation of Wells Fargo took a significant hit. And customers started to leave.

For Wells Fargo's competitors, it might have been easy to scoop up and swipe disgruntled Wells Fargo customers to their own banks. But the CEO of U.S. Bank, Richard Davis, whose bank could have readily profited by feasting on its wounded competitor, responded in ways consistent with the intention of Davis' "grandmother clause" (noted in Chapter 1). Davis forbid his employees from proactively pursuing any Wells Fargo accounts.

"We went out on Monday morning and asked everyone in the company to take no advantage of the Wells' circumstance," Davis said. "None."

The news media immediately picked up on Davis' sentiments about Wells Fargo, because he mentioned them publicly while attending a New York investor conference. Davis' timing was intentional, as that same day, Wells Fargo was just starting to be investigated by Congress.

Despite the opportunity to poach Wells Fargo customers, Davis was emphatic about holding true to a standard of business decency. "It's not our job to go out there and call that out," he said. "It would be inappropriate. And I don't think it would be the right way to do business."

Marcia Page, Founding Partner and Executive Chair at Värde, also operates in the financial services arena, where the ethics of hedge fund firms like hers is often questioned. She's seen the indiscretions of her peers play out in the business media in ways that also taint the reputation of the industry overall. She underscored the importance of demonstrating her values consistently and publicly as Richard Davis did–both inside Värde, as well as in the marketplace.

"We did the work early on to write down our values on paper, but soon after, I realized that if the employees weren't seeing the values modeled from the top, day in and day out, people will take their cues from what I do, not what we are asking them to do," Marcia Page said. "Actions are louder than words. And it's super,

super important to conduct yourself externally and internally in exactly the same way. That's what speaks the loudest."

Ironically, Greg Page (no relation to Marcia Page) had a similar observation, about leaders needing to "walk the talk" when it comes to ethics. "If you watch leaders long enough you will see a number of times where they tried to verbally lead their way out of something, instead of behaving their way out of it," Page said. "It's appalling. It sends a message to employees and everyone else that it's OK to be hypocritical and disingenuous and a whole host of other things. It's self-serving, and not at all ethical."

Not surprisingly, when he was CEO of Cargill, Page regularly reminded employees and customers of the company's iron clad Guiding Principles, published on the company's website for the entire world to view. The company rigorously enforces a no-exceptions standard to these Guiding Principles.

1. We obey the law.

2. We conduct our business with integrity.

3. We keep accurate and honest records.

4. We honor our business obligations.

5. We treat people with dignity and respect.

6. We protect Cargill's information, assets and interests.

7. We are committed to being a responsible global citizen.

Treating Employees as People First Attracts Good People

Here's where references to mothers and grandmothers comes alive again from the 15 leader interviews. If every leader has a maternal figure watching how employees are treated under their watch, employee engagement and trust would likely be much higher. My observation is that good leaders treat people the same way at work that they treat people at home, and vice-versa. Goodness, when shared, creates more goodness. It grows through sharing.

Gone are the days when the majority of employees went to work and blocked out what was going on in their personal lives. When people started carrying cellphones several years ago, they experienced a new sense of freedom because they could now suddenly stay in touch with family, friends, and work without needing to be planted near a landline phone. It was a renaissance of personal power. But that individual power was quickly usurped by companies when managers found mobile communication to be a source of untapped productivity.

Seemingly overnight, our personal mobile devices began to ping and buzz in our pockets, on our personal time, with work-related messages. Soon after, the daily details of our personal lives began to ping and buzz in our purses and pockets at work. Leaders who previously believed in creating a firewall between work life and home life were challenged to rethink their policies.

Within this new e-cultural backdrop is this reality: Employees perform at their best in the smartphone era when they feel supported as a person with a life outside of work. This is an employee dynamic that small business owners know especially well, because the positive (or negative) impact of any one employee is proportionately higher than in larger organizations. Additionally, the owner's personal finances are directly tied to the financial performance of the business.

We heard this theme from sandwich shop owner Dan Balach. Whether his business prospers or falters depends significantly on how the hourly employees believe they are treated. If his managers create a demeaning culture in the stores, employees will leave and sometimes go to work down the block in the same strip mall. And what do you think these ex-employees say to their new colleagues and customers about their former employer? It likely isn't complimentary. You can see how, when such events happen, it can directly impact productivity and the bottom line.

"You have to get to know employees in ways that are meaningful to them," said Colleen Needles Steward. "Because the employees are your link to your customers. And when they have important work, and big goals, they can get discouraged by any number of things–inside or outside of work. If you know them well, you will know how to be encouraging in ways that will help overcome the fear of failure, and help them keep their promises on the job. And that's huge."

Several other leaders we interviewed shared similar interests in getting to know their employees as individuals first. As noted earlier, when you treat employees positively, it has a beneficial ripple effect, which impacts how these employees interact with one another and your customers. It's smart business, and is a foundational piece of business ethics.

Karen Clark Cole, CEO at Blink UX, reminds her managers that the company's people-first strategy is clearly all about valuing employees, and ensuring they're able to provide positive results toward the business. "As the leader here, I feel like it's my responsibility to figure out what's going on when somebody's having a bad day," Clark Cole said. "It's about creating the right environment, where people know we care, so everyone is giving their best effort so we can thrive together."

Liz Smith, President at Assurance Agency, has a similar employee-centric story to share: "I'd say one of my secrets to ongoing success is that I try to learn something personal about each of the people on my team so it's not just a business relationship. I pride myself in knowing about their families and the things they enjoy outside of work. I think you've got to understand and know the 'whole' person to know what motivates each individual and adapt to that."

As employees feel valued by their employers, they extend those values to their respective family, social, and civic circles. The net benefit? Likely a far more vibrant, engaged, and uplifting community overall.

Policinski understands this dynamic well, as he formerly led a company in Land O'Lakes with more than 10,000 employees in locations throughout the United States. "What I've noticed is that getting to know the lives of your people is really important to ensuring they are engaged, because the successful companies have employees who are engaged," he said. "Engaged in what? Everything! They're at the Scouts. They're at the United Way. They're at the church or the Little League or the hockey rink. That's part of their business success, and part of their personal success. That's how people thrive in life. They're engaged in their families and in their communities."

"At Land O'Lakes, we want employees engaged in the schools, engaged politically, and socially," Policinski continued. "My observation is the great companies have the most engaged employees. I don't know if it's the chicken or the egg. If somehow great companies select engaged people and that's why the company is great, or great companies get people engaged in everything. It's probably a bit of both—we have to create a culture where people can thrive both personally and professionally for our business to be successful."

More Magnetic Ethics Insights

The importance of ethics in business was informed by multiple perspectives in the interviews, some of which are highlighted in these direct quotations:

- **Karen Clark Cole, CEO at Blink UX**: "Today, we need to let our employees bring their full selves to work. I take that really seriously. If we can have a truly happy employee who is valued as a whole person at work, then he or she feels like they are contributing in the world. And then they go home and are a better parent, friend, or neighbor. If we create that kind of environment, then we are helping our communities thrive as well. It all starts with helping the employees feel successful as people first."

- **Umit Nasifoglu, President at Wedding Day Diamonds**: "I think if you have a track record of being ethical and honest, it helps you even when you make a tough decision on people. They will respect your decision because they know you care. You're being good to them. It's totally unfair, and unethical, to not tell the truth to them in a difficult situation. They will see through it."

- **Liz Smith, President at Assurance Agency**: "As a leader, I live with the mantra 'be real.' The more approachable and relatable you are to your team, the stronger the team will be. I have found it is easier to have difficult conversations with people if you are transparent because they will have a greater level of trust and a greater understanding of your decisions."

The Skeptic's Shift

Paul Hillen

"Do we really need to tell people how to act and behave? Didn't their mothers teach them that?" said Martin Dudley, a senior manager at Cargill, when the two of us were having a discussion about what being "customer-focused" looked like. I replied, "Well, Martin, not all of us had the same mother." My point was, while we all think everyone around us knows the differences between right and wrong, or basic behavioral standards, we were all raised by different people with different lenses on the world. In organizations in which you have employees who have come from different companies and cultures, they will not only bring their personal values and ethics with them, but also those of the companies for whom they had previously worked.

So those of you who think clearly communicating your ethics isn't needed because, "Our mothers told us that" or "This is common sense stuff!" need to re-think your perspective. I should know, as I was once in that camp myself because of my personal and professional upbringing. I had the good fortune of having parents who were strong on what was right and wrong, unequivocally. I attended a Jesuit university where a course in business ethics was mandatory for getting a business degree. My first full-time job was at P&G, which had an unwavering code of ethical conduct. From all of these experiences, I just assumed everyone knew how to behave, but as we all know by reading or watching the news, that is not true.

When I got to Cargill and was exposed to the company's Guiding Principles, I questioned whether it was necessary to actually write down the first one: "We obey the law." Really, is that something we need to state, much less as the first one? Isn't that just known by everyone? Well, as I said, we weren't all raised by the same mother (or company). For an international company such as Cargill, with considerable business interests in countries with varying degrees of ethical compliance, I quickly learned how obeying the laws, or cultures of the land, was not something that could be taken for granted. Whether it was seeing Cargill's competitors engaging in ethical "shortcuts" like putting overweight trucks on the road, or outright bribery between these businesses and government officials, I saw how obeying the law could not be taken for granted.

This is why, especially for multi-national corporations that employ people from multiple cultures with different cultural norms, it is critical to write and articulate your clear expectations of what ethical behavior looks like in your organization. Or to be even clearer, spell out what ethical behavior "looks like" and "doesn't look like." This not only clarifies exactly your expectations, but also serves as a great tool for regularly discussing ethics with employees to ensure alignment.

Coaching Corner

How Can You Improve Your Magnetic Ethics?

☑ **Identify an ethics mentor to serve as a discussion and decision partner on ethical dilemmas.** Perhaps, like Greg Page, your partner could be a family member you do not wish to disappoint. Or find a colleague with whom you can discuss ethical matters. As Page suggests: "When facing a dilemma, employees are more likely to reach an ethical decision if they have a discussion with another colleague. Acting alone doesn't produce the same quality of decision-making." Or, your ethics mentor could be someone you don't know well but aspire to emulate. This could be someone real or fictional, alive or passed, famous or not, who can serve as a respected source in your inner conscience. Like the once-popular and ubiquitous WWJD bracelets ("What would Jesus do?"), you can create your own version of a "What would (fill in the blank) do?" ethical talisman or anchor.

☑ **Create a personal values framework, to help you role-model the behaviors aligned with your values.** If this idea is new to you, start by thinking about the values your family passed along to you. Write them down to see how they are alive in your leadership today. You may also decide to include the Cornerstones of Goodness, articulated in Chapter 2: Rewarding Excellence, Living Generously, Promoting Fairness, and Spreading Positivity. Growth in your leadership comes from creating a values framework for yourself, monitoring how well you live up to those values, and making the changes necessary to consistently role-model a values-based leadership style that other people you respect will consider ethical.

☑ **Do a people-first, workers-second audit by writing down the names of people inside and outside of work who are the most important to your success as a leader.** Assess for yourself–how much do you know about these people's lives outside of work? If you know very little, then identify a partner who has strong relationship skills to help you build a strategy to learn more about the people, in ways that are sincere, and won't be awkward.

CHAPTER 9
Summary: Why is Common Sense Not Common Practice?

"Do I believe goodness pays? Yes, in the perpetuation of the firm and the resilience of your brand and your reputation as an employer and a business partner. It's common sense."

Greg Page, Retired CEO and Chair at Cargill

In 2015, Paul Hillen and I set out to prove goodness pays financially in leadership. It's a relevant topic because our research before 2015 showed that four out of five leaders *believe* goodness pays. And yet only two of five are happy with the consistency of their financial results. There's a gap between those who believe it pays, and those who actually know how to make it pay. We wrote this book to help good leaders eliminate self-defeating habits, and to adopt a common-sense approach–centered on goodness–to create better business results.

Through this work, we successfully defined the connection between goodness and business leadership:

> Goodness in business is when people *thrive together* in a culture of encouragement, accountability, and positive teamwork.

Our most powerful finding was that *building a culture of goodness in leadership improves financial results.* Specifically, goodness pays financially when these Five Goodness Pays Factors come alive in leadership:

 Compelling business plan.
Prepare a business plan that creates genuine employee engagement and followership.

 Belief that profits are healthy for all.
Build commitment to the idea that profits are beneficial for everyone in the business–employees, executives, and owners.

 Team-based culture.
Create a culture that rewards a "we is greater than me" approach in which multiple people are accountable and rewarded for delivering on important promises.

 Timely and transparent decision-making.
Gain employee respect by making decisions in a timely fashion and by being accountable for the behaviors and results that come from those decisions.

 Magnetic ethics.
Attract good people by role modeling what is and what is not acceptable.

Throughout this book, you read qualitative and quantitative proof about *how* goodness pays, including coaching comments on how to make goodness pay specifically for you. This is valuable information, but you could also argue that some of it is nod-your-head-in-agreement common sense. In fact, throughout this project we often heard this reaction about goodness in leadership: *"I get that it's good to be good. I get that goodness makes a workplace healthier and more productive.* **I get it.**"

So if the principles of goodness are identified as sensible, why is this common sense not common practice? Why are there so many leaders without the Five Goodness Pays Factors present in their organizations?

Above-Average Blind Spot

Perhaps the root cause for how common sense is not common practice is what I call the "above-average effect." It's a cognitive bias that psychologists call *illusory superiority*. No one is immune. With the above-average effect, we believe our qualities and abilities in a given area are superior to those of others–even if that's likely untrue. With regard to leadership, it means many of us think we're better at leading with goodness than we actually are. Think of all of those who said they "get it"–about the idea of leading with goodness. But do they actually do it? There's a big difference between saying that you "get" goodness and regularly applying it to your leadership.

Studies on illusory superiority demonstrate the chasm between our often high self-opinion of our abilities and our actual performance. For example, one study showed that more than two-thirds of us believe we're better-than-average drivers–a statistical impossibility. In a separate study, 87% of Stanford MBA students rated their academic performance higher than the median performance of their peers. Again, statistically impossible.

Here's another example that hits closer to home for leaders: Research over many decades shows that most employees believe they can make decisions and perform to at least one level above their current pay grade. For some, it may be true. But most have incorrectly inflated opinions of their capabilities. This is supported by facts from search firms and private equity companies that less than 50% of leaders promoted to CEO succeed in the role beyond three years.

As a coach, I continually hear from clients about how they believe that one particular part of their job that's difficult for them in their current role will be easier "at the next level," because the talent around them will be better. But that makes no sense! It's exactly the same thing as a minor league baseball player, who struggles to hit a curve ball, but thinks it will be easier when he gets promoted to the major leagues, because the energy and encouragement of his big league teammates will somehow magically inspire better hitting.

The above-average effect occurs because we're lousy at objectively assessing our own qualities and abilities. Clara Shih, CEO at Hearsay Systems, shared her own perspective: "The biggest challenge I overcame as a leader was to realize I was putting business results above people and culture. I thought the best way to get good financial results was to focus on financial results," she reflected. "It took some on-the-job learning from people around me to realize first, that's the wrong priority order. And second, the two go hand in hand. If you invest in having really good people and you have a culture that's both caring and performance-oriented, then the business results sort themselves out."

Shih's insights open up the idea that the self-assessment is ongoing and comes from seeking out the observations of others. In other words, we might think we already know the principles of the Five Goodness Pays Factors, but we need to ask the people around us whether or not we are actually putting them into practice.

A Quick Way to Measure

In Chapter 3, I shared how, based on the detailed findings from the research, financial results can be predicted by a one-question survey–the Goodness Pays Score (GPS). The GPS is similar to the popular one-question Net Promoter Score (NPS) in how it can be administered and interpreted through any survey device. It's an easy way to check your above-average bias. Your actual GPS is calculated based on the average of your employee responses to this *one question*:

> *Using a 1-10 scale: How would you rate your direct leader on proactively promoting goodness in his/her decision-making within your organization?*

Based on our quantitative research for *How Goodness Pays*, we found that survey respondents who gave their leader a score of 9 or 10 on <u>this question</u> more often indicate their organization has increased its revenues under this leader. In fact, 81% of those who scored a 9 or 10 on this question reported an increase in year-over-year revenue, while 18% saw revenue stay the same versus the previous year.

The GPS segments the average score into three categories:

1. GPS = 9-10, Your company is led by managers who are *Goodness Accelerators*

2. GPS = 7-8, Your company is led by managers who are *Goodness Neutral*

3. GPS = 1-6, Your company is led by managers who are *Goodness Drainers*

Chapter 3 also provides specific recommendations for how leaders can improve in each of the categories, which align with the Coaching Corner suggestions in Chapters 4-8.

Common Sense: What Gets In the Way?

When speaking on the subject of goodness in leadership and business, many people ask "Isn't this just common sense?" The answer is yes. The second question is "What do you think are the major barriers to goodness–what gets in the way?" Some of these questioners are looking for me to say something that does not describe themselves, like *greed, evil, or enjoying profiting at the expense of others.* Then they can think *"Whew, at least that doesn't describe me!"* But that's not what I think, because most people are not intrinsically bad.

Keep in mind that in earlier chapters I shared research on how human beings are exponentially more motivated by helping people, not hurting them. That tells me that those whom others might describe as "bad leaders" most likely are that way because they truly believe, in their own chosen leadership styles, that they are actually helping their employees. Yes, believe it or not. That's why you so often hear "bad leaders" say something like "I had no idea" when confronted with their sub-optimal leadership style.

The most common enemy of goodness in leadership is short-term thinking. It's what causes leaders to go against their better selves and start to falsely think: *"I don't have any choice in this situation. We have to get results now, so I have to do it this way."* It's those two words, "have to," that self-justify the small and large decisions that contradict goodness:

- "I don't really want to yell at him in front of his colleagues, but I **have to** or else he won't know not to do it again."

- "The reason I don't ask them about this major decision, even though I told them I would, is that I simply **have to** get it done by the end of the week."

- "Why should I **have to** take the time to explain this to her? If I **have to** do this for everyone, I won't have any time to get my other work done!"

Over time, if these contradictory "have to" behaviors are reinforced by mentors and supervisors, leaders learn that command-and-control or belittling leadership styles are the best ways to get results in "the real world." That style becomes their habit. And suddenly, out of the blue, a "bad leader" is born. It's unfortunate because it doesn't need to be this way.

Breaking Through to Goodness

We know old habits are hard to break. Repeating old habits feels better because it's easier and faster. But the longer we repeat those habits, the more inertia builds up and we increase the size of our blind spots. Blind spots are biases and bad habits that simply haven't been brought to the surface of our awareness. All leaders have blind spots, but those blind spots don't mean a leader has bad intentions.

> *All leaders have blind spots, but those blind spots don't mean a leader has bad intentions.*

Consider the famous Duke University popcorn study. The study participants were sent to a movie theater and told they would be asked about what attracts people to the movies. Instead, everyone received a box of popcorn while the movie played. Some boxes had freshly made popcorn; others had stale, rubbery, week-old popcorn. Those who rarely ate popcorn at the movies stayed away from eating the bad popcorn. Those who habitually ate popcorn while viewing a movie gobbled up the week-old popcorn, even though they later admitted it tasted bad. Because these people couldn't sit still in a movie theater without eating popcorn–even bad popcorn–they allowed their habit to overrule their logical, sensible decision-making. Old habits are really hard to break.

Based on our firm's experience coaching and mentoring hundreds of executives, there are three main reasons why leaders don't confront their habits, identify their biases and blind spots, and fully lead with goodness:

1. **Fear.** Leaders are afraid that exhibiting and practicing goodness will not actually work, or worse yet, they will be belittled or somehow it will be used against them.

2. **External influences.** Leaders get swept away by uncontrollable events in their personal and professional lives, and by the influence of people they can't resist.

3. **Change is difficult**. Frankly, it's hard to change yourself, and it's hard to change the culture around you. But that doesn't mean it can't be done.

If any of the reasons listed above apply to you or someone you know, the good news is that they are all possible to overcome. The first step is recognizing the need to change a detrimental habit and replace it with a new learned behavior that creates better results.

Overcome Your Fears about Goodness

Fear is an influential component in our decision-making. Nobel Prize-winning behavioral economist Daniel Kahneman says we typically fear losing twice as much as we relish success. *What if I fail?* The repercussions of failure can cripple leaders' wisdom and leave them in the dark. And, frequently, leaders don't even actively realize their decision-making is based in fear.

The first step to overcoming fear is to tap into our aspirational muscles and imagine business outcomes that are almost beyond our wildest dreams. Psychology research confirms one of the most powerful ways to help us overcome our natural inclination for negativity and hard-to-break habits is by having a vivid and compelling goal. Aspirations are vivid and compelling goals. And aspirations give us hope, confidence, and a motivational push to try new things–all important to goodness in leadership. For example, striving to become an inspirational leader, whom other leaders admire and regularly consult for advice, will likely serve as a great catalyst to learn more about inspirational leadership and will start you on the path to becoming exactly that kind of leader.

The push-back we get from skeptics about having goodness and aspirations is driven by a mindset along the lines of "goodness is fluffy BS." These reactions always fall into one of three categories, which I call the fear-based *myths* about goodness.

Myth #1: Goodness is a religious term that has no place in business. Yes, most religions share some version of goodness as a virtue–but as stated earlier, our research shows that four out of five business leaders believe goodness pays, when goodness is defined as *people believing they can thrive together.* Most people are sick of the "dark noise" that surrounds us in the modern world, and find a discussion about goodness to be refreshing and inspiring.

Myth #2: Goodness is soft, and can't be measured or managed. The people who measure perception and employee engagement would not agree. And with the emergence of business watchdog sites online like Glassdoor.com and ConsumerWatchdog.com, your business reputation is anything but soft. If you lead with goodness, the best talent and customers will gravitate to you, and stay with you. If not, your costs of replacing employees and customers will soar.

Myth #3: Goodness gets exploited. Radiating goodness does not mean you are a leader who is easily bullied. In fact, employing honesty, fairness, and ethical decision-making almost always requires standing your ground–not caving in the face of opposition. Goodness is hard work.

For some leaders, in their desperation for achieving short-term results, fear can cause them to become blinded to the long-term impacts of their behaviors. Part of the problem is that short-term behaviors like aggression and sky-is-falling thinking can create immediate results. People regularly cite examples of high-profile leaders who got rich by bullying people in their firms. But those are the unsustainable exception, not the rule. When a normally-charismatic leader is suddenly shouting or growling at employees in team meetings, it sure makes an immediate impression, but at the long-term expense of goodness.

The wounds from short-term thinking can scar an organization for years to come.

As Chris Policinski, the retired CEO at Land O'Lakes, observed, the wounds from short-term thinking can scar an organization for years to come: "There are a lot of folks who take shortcuts to drive performance, and there's nowhere to hide, really. In any one month, or quarter, or year, or short period of time, you can take that shortcut. But over time, those shortcuts come to light: 'I've trashed the environment.' Well, that'll come out. 'I've cut product quality.' That'll come out. 'I treat my employees poorly.' Well, you're going to get what you deserve."

Goodness evaporates when leaders run *from* a fear instead of *toward* their aspirations. Teams lose their dedication and motivation when they sense their leader is running from a fear. They thrive when decisions and investments are made for the benefit of long-term growth, rather than due to an immediate fear. As an acclaimed corporate leader, who led a widely admired company, Policinski knows this firsthand: "Companies that endure have this long-term point of view and vision for their leadership. It's an ethical way to approach business."

Minimize Negative External Influences

Aspirational leadership naturally puts pressure on those who have aggressive growth expectations. As we continuously strive for bigger and better results for ourselves and those around us, we can unintentionally create new problems:

- Investing in exciting new product development or marketing strategies puts pressure on cash flow, a common business problem.

- Increasing expectations likely causes some leaders to struggle or leave; without bench strength, that's a common problem.

- Pursuing and winning a huge new customer puts pressure on work/life blending when the surge of new work takes over the firm; if the surge lasts too long, it creates problems of bitterness or burnout.

- Getting promoted into your dream job automatically creates new demands on your time, energy, and ability to effectively handle bigger decisions; any of these can cause relationship problems, both inside and outside of work.

Whether issues like these are brought to our attention by family members, friends, bosses, or colleagues, it can be tempting to take the easy way out, such as cutting corners, handling emotional situations without empathy, and covering up the truth. But these only create more problems in the future. Dealing with the inevitable negative repercussions of decisions made from short-term thinking motivated by fear almost always proves more difficult than doing things the right way to start.

Frequently clients share some version of saying: "The routines of my day-to-day life keep me from doing the things I'd like to do or should do." Daily tasks and unexpected demands can pull even the most efficient leaders toward the lowest common denominator tasks, unless they're handled appropriately. As veteran business executive Paul Hillen explains: "Most people in business are so busy with the day-to-day work that they don't spend the time thinking through the strategic impact of their work. They get pulled down into daily problem-solving and don't spend the time to learn the craft, shape the vision, and help others learn from research."

The daily problem-solving doesn't only happen at work. Often, we're distracted by the problems of others through the "dark noise" of the news media or dealing with personal issues affecting friends or family members. The negativity tests our elasticity. Because modern schedules rarely include sufficient time for us to reflect on our own health, well-being, and personal satisfaction, we sometimes lose sight of the need for self-care. Every leader can benefit from better self-care to lessen the potentially harsh impact of outside influences.

Overcome the Difficulty of Change

You may have heard this before: "People don't like change, even when it's positive." Thousands of books have been published on the subject of change in the workplace, and *change management* is a prolific segment of the management consulting industry. What these books and consultants teach us is that, even a workplace strategy as seemingly positive as goodness, can, and likely will, threaten someone, because it represents change.

"Perhaps the biggest problem with common sense is that it falls prey to the clear limits of personal experience," writes Jim Taylor, PhD, author of "The Power of Prime" in *Psychology Today*. What Taylor means is that people who've had a negative experience with changes in leadership of any kind will focus on their previous negative experience, despite the possibility of the current situation becoming positive.

You've probably heard the term "skittish" used to describe animals such as horses, dogs, or cats who seem nervous or excitable. Typically, the skittish behaviors have nothing to do with these animals' current owners or handlers; they're more likely due to a prior, negative life experience. The same dynamic, based on prior experience, often happens in humans. It's based on the reality that people are hard-wired to defend what they already know, even if what they already know doesn't serve them well.

Paul Hillen has specific insight on the difficulty of change, even when it is seemingly sensible: "When I suggest to sales people that they spend more time asking questions about their customers' business, I get a lot of nodding heads. But then I ride with those sales people, and they spend 90% of the time talking about their own company and not the customer's company. They usually take a canned presentation and change the logo, rather than digging deep in to their customer beforehand and asking questions about a strategy or decision during the meeting."

Why can't otherwise seemingly sensible adults more readily accept change, even when they know it's a positive? The short answer is this: We only change if and when we want to change. We can only begin to change when we develop a new desire for better things in our lives–better relationships, better financial results, better health, or a better outlook for the future. So, if you are inspired to make some changes in your leadership, which you believe will be better for everyone, don't get caught off guard by unexpected resistance. It's not personal–it's human nature.

The Pathway to Goodness: The Seven Fs

Leading with goodness is hard work. It takes energy to push back our intrinsic personal and professional instincts toward selfish behaviors. And don't kid yourself–we all have them! Creating an others-orientation so that people can *thrive together* requires physical, emotional, and intellectual strength. That's why our firm invented a holistic and highly popular life and leadership model called The Seven Fs to help leaders live with less stress and lead with less fear. Good leadership comes from the strength that can be gained by blending the Seven Fs, which are: faith, family, finances, fitness, friends, fun and future.

The definitions of the Seven Fs are:

1. **Faith**—How satisfied are you with your spiritual life? (Note: this does not necessarily need to mean "faith" in a traditional religious sense; your definition of faith is up to you.)

2. **Family**—How satisfied are you with your loved ones who share a common sense of home?

③ **Finances**—How satisfied are you with how your money funds your priorities?

④ **Fitness**—How satisfied are you with the health of your body?

⑤ **Friends**—How satisfied are you with the people who share your joys and disappointments?

⑥ **Fun**—How satisfied are you with the part of your life that is playful and joyful?

⑦ **Future**—How satisfied are you with the hope you have for yourself and others?

Remember the "F'n Do-Gooder" reference in Chapter 1? The anonymous e-mailer was taking a shot at my use of The Seven Fs as a foundational element of leadership. When he asked: "What are you, an F'n Do-Gooder?" my conclusion was, "Yes!"

But now, nearly eight years later, I've come to a deeper conclusion: It's easier for leaders to radiate goodness if their lives are in a good place. When they have positive momentum on their faith, family, finances, fitness, friends, fun and future, they have a sense of positivity that radiates outward to the people important to their success. And they build the inner confidence of being able to do the right things in difficult situations.

A simple way to assess where your life is at *right now* is to self-assess with what we call the Seven Fs Wheel. It's a simple way of measuring what the ancient Egyptians figured out 4,000 years ago–the connection of mind, body, and spirit is a powerful and important part of a good life–and goodness in leadership.

Here's how the Seven Fs Wheel works:

On the wheel printed here, you will find seven spokes, each corresponding with one of The Seven Fs. Based on the definitions of The Seven Fs listed previously, assess your satisfaction on a 1-10 scale, with "10" being the highest satisfaction, and "1" being the lowest satisfaction. There are no right or wrong answers, rather, this is an exercise to help you be intellectually honest about these important things in your life and leadership.

The Seven Fs Wheel

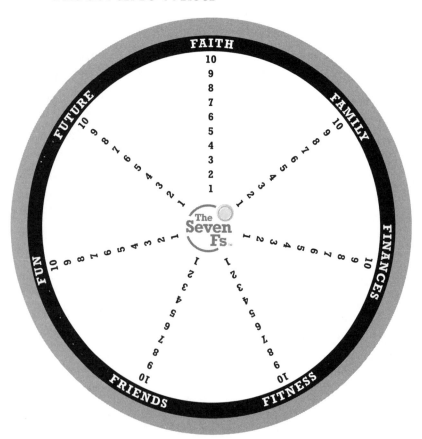

The fun starts when you connect the dots to form the shape of your Seven Fs Wheel. And then, you can ask yourself the question: *"Does my Seven Fs Wheel roll?"*

As a leader, paying attention to the shape of your "wheel" and the momentum you have on each of the Seven Fs can help you be true to what's going on in your life. It's an authentic way to lead, which is perhaps the most in-demand leadership quality today. People appreciate and gravitate toward authentic leaders who lead a blended, happy, and holistic life.

You can learn more specifically about the Seven Fs and how to apply them to your life in the book, *What Really Works,* by Paul Batz and Tim Schmidt (2011, Beaver's Pond Press).

In Summary

Good leaders create great results by leading with goodness. It's an others-centric orientation, and reflective of an ability to maintain a healthy tension between taking a long-term view and having short-term performance expectations. Goodness pays financially for leaders who embrace the Five Goodness Pays Factors in their leadership:

 Compelling business plan.
Prepare a business plan that creates genuine employee engagement and followership.

 Belief that profits are healthy for all.
Build commitment to the idea that profits are beneficial for everyone in the business–employees, executives, and owners.

 Team-based culture.
Create a culture that rewards a "we is greater than me" approach in which multiple people are accountable and rewarded for delivering on important promises.

Timely and transparent decision-making.
Gain employee respect by making decisions in a timely fashion and by being accountable for the behaviors and results that come from those decisions.

 Magnetic ethics.
Attract good people by role modeling what is and what is not acceptable.

The rewards of leading with goodness are measurable: consistently positive financial results, stronger relationships with the people important to your success, and a stronger sense of purpose in your work. And maybe the best pay-off: leading with goodness will help you work with a clean heart and mind, knowing you are *radiating goodness* every day.

Karen Clarke Cole, CEO at Blink UX, put it best when she articulated the rewards of leading with goodness:

"If you treat your employees with value and respect, they're going to be more productive, and your business ultimately more profitable. I never want to be the kind of leader who is out of touch with the work and her employees. For me, it's about creating the right environment so that our people can thrive, they're getting feedback and they're clear on their roles and responsibilities. If our employees feel like they're positively contributing to the world, then they go home at the end of the day feeling valued, and they're in turn a better husband, wife, parent and neighbor."

So, are you ready to radiate goodness today?

Connect with Us

I hope to continue the *How Goodness Pays* conversation with you. Please connect with us on Linked In, or by email: **info@goodleadership.com.**

About Good Leadership Enterprises

Good Leadership Enterprises is a leadership consulting boutique with world-class strategies to help executive teams exceed their goals, both personally and professionally. The firm's brand of good leadership is based on the art and science of working together to produce great results. And it starts with the idea: Goodness Pays. Headquartered in Minneapolis, Minnesota, the firm serves local, national, and international clients through a consortium of highly experienced coaching partners who represent best-in-class in their areas of expertise. Clients appreciate a personalized client experience, research-based proprietary tools, inspiring retreats and events, and coaches who help them grow both personally and professionally. Founded in 2009 by Paul and Melinda Batz, the firm has grown year after year, fueled by their belief that goodness pays, because goodness grows. The firm's signature book, *How Goodness Pays*, provides a research-based blueprint for good leaders who want to create healthy growth in their enterprises. Learn more at www.goodleadership.com.

About Paul Batz

Paul Batz is a thought leader on how goodness pays in leadership and business, and recognized as one of the top leadership bloggers in America. He is an author, executive coach, and international speaker who built his firm, Good Leadership Enterprises, with the same strategies around goodness he teaches clients. His firm is a leadership consulting boutique with world-class strategies to coach executive teams with bold aspirations how to exceed their goals, both personally and professionally. He has created several books on leadership, including the bestselling book, *What Really Works,* and the latest title, *How Goodness Pays.*

About Paul Hillen

Paul Hillen is an accomplished senior business executive with 32 years of experience in general management, sales management and marketing, at both large, multi-national companies (Procter & Gamble, Cargill) and at mid/small size companies. He has held positions as President, Chief Operating Officer, Senior Vice President, Chief Commercial Officer, and Chief Marketing Officer. Paul currently has the role of President and Chief Operating Officer at Revier Brand Group, LLC at Revier Cattle Company. He has received numerous awards for business and marketing expertise, including being chosen as one of the top 100 most talented Global Marketing Leaders by the World Marketing Congress, and one of the globe's top CMOs by the CMO Club. He is also an author, speaker, and serves as a board member for non-profit and for profit organizations. Hillen has also served on advisory boards at the University of Chicago Booth School of Business and the Carlson School of Management at the University of Minnesota.